A CALLED CREATIVES COMPILATION

PEACE
BE
WITH
YOU

STORIES OF GOD'S HOPE AND
HEALING FOR WEARY HEARTS

Library of Congress Cataloging-in-Publication Data

LCCN: 2026905981 (paperback) ISBN: 978-1-961732-32-2 (ebook) | ISBN: 978-1-961732-33-9 (paperback) | ISBN: 978-1-961732-34-6 (hardcover)

Published in association with Called Creatives Publishing, www.calledcreativespublishing.com, Gallatin, TN

Cover design: Called Creatives Publishing
Interior design: Called Creatives Publishing
Interior Formatting: Dallas Hodge

TABLE OF CONTENTS

INTRODUCTION

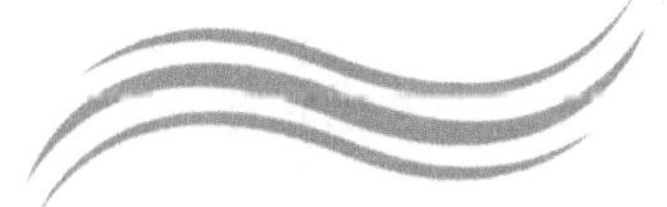

In a world filled with uncertainty and noise, peace can feel out of reach.

Our days are often chaotic, and many of us have been sold a version of peace—one that looks like a feeling, a means of control, or a reward for figuring it all—that doesn't hold up under pressure.

That kind of peace doesn't last. Temporary peace is built on circumstances which have a habit of shifting.

The peace of God works differently. It doesn't require calm seas or answered questions. It's not something we manufacture through enough quiet time or the right mindset. It's found in a Person, and He meets us in our mess.

The women whose writing you will read in these pages know this, firsthand. They are writers from the Called Creatives community, and they are remarkably gifted. But more than that, they are honest. They've written about real seasons of waiting, grief, doubt, and unexpected turns. They've told the truth about what it feels like when life doesn't cooperate with your plans.

And in every story, you'll find the same thread: God was there. Not distant or disappointed, but present, faithful, and near. Bringing a peace that passes all understanding in the midst of real life.

Our hope is that you'll recognize yourself somewhere in these pages; that something written will feel like it was meant for you. And that by the time you turn the last page, you'll know a little more deeply that peace isn't something you chase. It's Someone who has already found you.

APRON STRINGS OF PEACE

Cindy Bennett

The kitchen was the warmest room in our old farmhouse, the center of everything familiar and safe. The air smelled like baked casserole crust, comfort, and home all wrapped together.

But one cold morning in that same kitchen, everything changed.

Dad stood at the door with his luggage, saying he was going on a trip (he was a trucker) and that he'd be back. But something in me knew this time was different. My heart sank. My little brothers, one still in diapers, near the sidelights watching, too young to grasp the weight of the moment. I didn't know it then, but that moment left a quiet mark on me. One that still shapes how mercy rises in my heart today, and how I've come to understand the kind of peace only Jesus can give.

Life shifted quickly. That winter, we pulled down the red old-fashioned drapes and hung them in the dining room to keep the heat in. With the oven door cracked open and a blanket stretched across the floor vent, my siblings and I huddled underneath to catch the warmth. It was somehow still good: all of us together in one space while the bedrooms of the farmhouse sat empty.

I remember Mom in the kitchen, making cozy meals. At any moment, one of us could run up for help or a quick hug. She modeled gentle strength and optimism.

Eventually, Mom had to work outside the home, but she still made sure we caught the church bus each week. When Mom remarried, the home I'd known began to feel different. An unsettledness stirred.

I didn't know where to take the ache. So when that first sip of something sweet met my weary heart, it set me on a path toward binge drinking. By college, my Bible sat untouched, and Sundays were for sleeping in.

I felt like the prodigal, stuck in my own pigpen, chasing anything that promised relief, distraction, or belonging. But even in my wandering, God never let go.

Eventually, the hurt I kept trying to outrun caught up with me. One morning in my mid-twenties, everything surfaced. I found myself kneeling in my living room between my cats, Jasmine and Belle, heart open.

No spotlights, just an honest conversation. And in that moment, I surrendered my life to Jesus. He met me with a Father's tenderness I didn't see coming and stitched peace into the torn places I thought would never heal.

Slowly, clarity came. God opened my eyes to the truth woven into those apron strings. The calm of my childhood had always been His love flowing through her. As a young mom left alone with five children, she carried more than I understood. Still, she kept showing up, cooking, serving, and finding her way as Jesus led her. It wasn't perfect, but it was holy and good.

As the years went on, the closeness Mom and I once shared settled into something quieter. Still there, just stretched between longer pauses and check-ins.

Two years ago, God nudged me to reach out to Mom, not knowing what was coming. We talked for an hour as she filled me in, focusing on everyone else before herself. When I finally asked, "Mom, how are you?" she paused. That's when she shared she hadn't been feeling well and might have cancer.

That April, her diagnosis was confirmed. And in her usual way, she shared what she had to.

As treatment began, God drew us into the tender work of caring for Mom the way she once cared for us: laying aside her apron as we picked up a serving towel. Each of us loved her in our own way, and it drew us closer.

From simple manicures to placing her orange flowers on the porch, to fixing the door handle, to bringing coffee on long days, to cooking her favorite meals: every act became a thread in her care. One of the sweetest moments was watching my sis-in-love, Tami, bring Mom homemade applesauce, apples simmered with cloves. After weeks of hospital food, that little bowl of comfort helped her pills go down easier.

Each act sacred. Holy. A gift.

I flew back and forth from Florida to Michigan to be by Mom's bedside. Seeing her strength and voice fade was so, so hard. All I wanted was for her to rest in the kind of peace she'd once wrapped around us in that farmhouse kitchen. Those hours with her were an unexpected gift: a time to lay old hurts down, see each other clearly again, and make peace with the parts of our story that had gone unspoken.

In those final days, we gathered around her bedside, sharing bowls of her famous goulash. Two days later, on a Valentine's weekend she would've loved, Mom surrendered her apron to the One who welcomed her home.

Grief continued quietly, just as it had for months before she passed. In the weeks that followed, her legacy met me in ordinary places: birthday parties, best-loved recipes, the warmth of home. I didn't see the gift of those apron strings growing up, but now I know they were grace doing quiet, unseen work.

Losing Mom taught me what I couldn't see as a child: how the smallest acts of love can shape a life. And that kind of love is for your story, too.

"You will keep in perfect peace those whose minds are steadfast, because they trust in You" (Isaiah 26:3).

No matter where you find yourself, full of hope or weighed down, peace doesn't come from a settled life. It comes from Jesus who keeps you steady. And if the road feels heavy for you or a loved one, don't underestimate the power of showing up. Love offered in hard moments invites a peace that lasts.

Jesus meets us in every tiny yes, one loosely tied apron string at a time.

Good night, sweet Mama, apron strings came undone.
We knew not to tie them back, as we trust you to the One.

Cindy Bennett is a pastor's wife and mom of four who loves helping women see Jesus in their everyday moments. She creates mini devotionals and Bible studies. Cindy leads Pathway Women in Vero Beach and enjoys slow days, family time, and soaking up time with her first grandbaby, Alora Dove.

REDEFINING HOME:
A JOURNEY THROUGH LOSS, FAITH, AND PEACE

Duffy Betterton

Strapped down to a body board with a neck brace on, I was lying in the emergency room waiting for my mom to arrive. At 17, I had totaled my car. I hit the windshield with my forehead; blood covered my face and ruined my new outfit. I held onto my keychain, the only thing left from my car, knowing somehow that I would be okay. I wondered why God had saved me and what He had planned for me. Being spared made me face a deeper longing in me: a need for a steady place to belong, something my heart had chased for years. As a child of divorced parents, I had two families that loved me well during my teen years, yet there was a lingering hunger for purpose and a place to call home.

Two weeks later, I was standing before a group of third and fourth graders. My forehead was raw, with little glass shards waiting to work themselves out. My bangs covered the physical wound, but my heart was still raw. It was my turn to tell the kids the crucifixion story and how much Jesus loved them. We had already made our craft for the day, a keychain cross made of carpenter's nails. As I shared the literal Word of God with the children (John 1:1), I held that same keychain from the accident, and I was flooded with a peace that said, "This is your Home. I am your Home. Sharing about me draws you closer to Home." That moment planted a seed in me: a calling to dwell in Him and serve Him with my life.

One year later, I set out for college, feeling called to a life of service through missions. I trusted that God had given me two families that loved Him. I thought I knew the shape of my future. But just as I stepped out on what I thought home meant to me, both of my parents' marriages fell apart.

Anger and frustration returned as I struggled to redefine home again. Fear held me back from trusting others. Surrounded by people, I was at first numb and then alone behind walls built by anger and fear, not letting anyone in to really love me or even see my hurt. Recklessly dating the bad guys and shutting out the good guys and friends brought me to a desperate cry to God. Why would He allow my parents to remarry, give my brothers the same doubts and fears I faced, and let me feel secure in relationships that would fail? If the places I had defined as good were failing, where could I find home?

Could I trust Him to be my home when He allowed my families to be ripped apart? A deep ache of "why" resounded in my heart and mind. *Lord, where are you and why did you allow this to happen?*

But God kept pursuing me. He had been teaching me about His faithfulness. Even though I wasn't willing to trust people, He surrounded me with those who spoke His Word over me.

Psalm 23 became a gentle echo, drawing me closer to a God who would provide, guide, protect, and give me a place to dwell, in relationship with Him. "Surely your goodness and love will follow me all the days of my life, and I will dwell in the house of the Lord forever" (Psalm 23:6).

Those words didn't just sound familiar. They felt personal. I remember reading this during my college years and crumpling into tears. I so desperately wanted a place where goodness and love would follow me.

I wanted a place to call home, a safe place to dwell.

A place where I was not trying to define relationships.

A place that I didn't have to fear would fall apart.

A place where one person couldn't make a decision that would change my foundation.

A safe place to lie down and know that when I got up, it would be the same; where the rules were solid and unchanging.

A place that wouldn't leave me.

A place where home was defined.

Even as Psalm 23 drew me closer to Him, my heart still longed for peace. Philippians 4:6-7 became my heart's cry and my salve. "Do not be anxious about anything, but in every situation, by prayer and petition, with thanksgiving, present your requests to God. And the peace of God, which transcends all understanding, will guard your hearts and your minds in Christ Jesus" (Philippians 4:6-7).

I was yearning for this peace. I wanted a peace that surpassed understanding, but I certainly didn't have it. I was mad, hurt, and confused. I wanted something that would guard my heart and mind.

So I backed up to verse 6: in every situation, ask God with thanksgiving (Philippians 4:6).

Okay, Lord, this is hard. I'm tired of looking for home. I'm tired of trusting people only to be disappointed. I'm tired of trying to find my way. I don't understand why divorce had to happen, again! Can you fix it? Will you fix it? Will you be my home? Will you give me that peace so I can stop looking for it?

Do you know what His answer was?

"Yes, daughter, I've already done it. Read the last phrase of verse 7: 'in Christ Jesus' (Philippians 4:7). I had a plan for you. I have given you myself through my Son. You don't have to worry or look for home anymore. I love you so much that I made a way for you to be part of my family. I am your provider. I am your answer. I am your Home."

It is the same message I heard as I shared about Him after my accident, and it still resounds. The Lord used my parents' divorce(s) to teach me about His faithfulness, His character, and His desire to be my satisfaction. As I searched for that place, He loved me through His Word, showing me that He is the home I longed for then and now.

Redefining home is a journey of wrapping truth, God's Word, around the life He has given us. It is finding our satisfaction and peace in the One who not only created us but also gave Himself for us so we walk with Him and share Him with others. He wants to be our Home.

God's Word answers the questions and quiets our hearts.

He and His Word are our peace, our Home.

Duffy Betterton is a wife, mom, and business owner who leads, serves, and dances. Gratefully married for more than 26 years and shaped by her story as a child of divorce, she seeks to build community and help others find deep rest in the generous love of a faithful God.

HARDSCRABBLE FAITH

Jody Bickett

I could smell the pine needles in the heat. It was dry, every summer was dry, and the pine needles smelled like they might just burst into flames. We had been driving for an hour, lumbering up the road in the old Ram, leaving a cloud of dust behind us. We rounded the bend and to the left was the wide expanse of the valley below us and to the right was the parking lot of the Hardscrabble Cafe. We parked in front of the restaurant, but it was closed. They couldn't make it through the summer, and had locked the doors before the season was over. My grandpa wanted to get out to stretch and peek in the windows to see what might have been. The parking lot was full of dirt and gravel, and I could feel dust starting to collect under the straps of my new sandals. I worried that the mix of dust and sweat would stain them, that when I moved my toes people would see how dirty they were.

My grandma looked around and said, "I guess they weren't hardscrabble enough to make it up here." The wind started to blow, my bangs whipped across my eyes, and between the dust and the dry heat (and my general fear that the forest might catch fire at any moment) I was ready to climb back into the truck and sit between my grandparents. As if reading my mind, Grandma smiled and said, "You, my dear, are very hardscrabble."

Hardscrabble? What did that even mean? At eight, I wasn't sure, but it felt like a compliment in a world full of obstacles. In Idaho, in the Rocky Mountains, a lot of life was hardscrabble, and the land had a way of reminding you what "hardscrabble" really meant—every season, every job, every rock underfoot.

In high school, I got a job at a dude ranch and at the start of the summer, we had to gather rocks from the horse corral. We picked rocks that had thrust themselves to the surface over the winter, springing up from the earth. It feels like life is this way: rocks just coming up from the depths of life, suddenly appearing as a trip hazard, an annoyance, a new task to be completed.

I did wonder if some people lived on smooth ground, lush grass underneath. In college, I had a friend from a wealthy family, and she approached life as if it were going to work out for her. She walked into everything with the mindset that it was all going to be okay, better than okay, it was great. Meanwhile, I was over here with my head down looking for rocks about to come to the surface. She was looking up, eyes on the horizon. What would that be like? To have all the resources? To take the risks knowing that if it didn't work out you would still be okay? I was envious of her calm. It was like she had a string pulling her up to heaven. She was tethered to the sky, and my string tethered me to earth's rocky soil.

I took the hardscrabble moniker that my grandma meant as a compliment and turned it into a definition of my circumstances. An overwhelming burden of tough times and hard work. It is impossible to find peace when you take your eyes off God and look to your own circumstances, hardscrabble or lush pastures. My natural tendency is to look at my own circumstances, head down. I have to remind myself to look up and to see all of the grace and goodness that Jesus provides. When I turn to the Lord and truly seek him, He answers me. He calls me His daughter. My Father is the wealthiest one of all, the creator of all the universe. My circumstances don't define me, Jesus defines me. It's hard to remember some days with a mountain of tasks to complete, dinners to prepare, emails to answer, children to raise. Sometimes it feels like all of life is about to be set on fire and I can feel that tether start to pull downward, my shoulders pulling in. This overwhelming feeling is a reminder to lift my eyes towards Jesus and focus on Him.

What I didn't know was that freedom wouldn't come from having more resources. It would come from a change in perspective, one only God could give. How do I tether myself to Jesus? The best way I've found is to tie myself to the Bible, wrapping these words around my heart.

His Word promises so many good things:

Tethered to the Lord: "Have I not commanded you? Be strong and courageous. Do not be afraid; do not be discouraged, for the Lord your God will be with you wherever you go" (Joshua 1:9).

Tethered to peace: "Come to terms with God and be at peace; in this way good will come to you. Receive instruction from his mouth, and place his sayings in your heart" (Job 22:21-22 CSB).

Tethered to His care: "The Lord is good, a refuge in times of trouble. He cares for those who trust in him" (Nahum 1:7).

And the one I repeat all the time:

Tethered to a calm mind and heart: "Do not be anxious about anything, but in every situation, by prayer and petition, with thanksgiving, present your requests to God. And the peace of God, which transcends all understanding, will guard your hearts and your minds in Christ Jesus" (Philippians 4:6-7).

This peace doesn't come from better circumstances or from tomorrow when things will supposedly slow down, but from my belief in Jesus. It comes from my relationship with Him, from my understanding that

He is in control. Sometimes it takes fervent prayers in the middle of the night to calm my mind. Also, I do better when I'm consistent in reading my Bible and when I spend time praising Him. It's a choice every day, and some days I make better choices than others. But through it all, God is faithful.

The rocks will still rise to the surface, but now I know who walks beside me, guiding me through them or helping me pick them up. Either way, I just need to keep my eyes on Him.

Jody Bickett was born and raised in Boise, Idaho, but has called Texas home for more than half her life. Married for 30 years with three wonderful children. For her day job she sells organic sugar to food manufacturers but spends her free time writing, water skiing, and spending time with friends and family.

SETTING PEACE FREE

Weslynn Biggers

"God, I can't handle You taking anything else."

The prayer came out raw in the pre-dawn darkness. I sat curled on the couch with my coffee, waiting for the sunrise while my family slept. Another 5 a.m. wake-up. Another morning of fear.

"I've lost enough. Haven't You asked enough from me? I'm afraid of what's to come next."

It would be months before He answered. Months of wrestling in the darkness.

The business my husband and I had built was declining, and with it, every plan we'd mapped out for our future. At the beginning of that decline, God asked us to relocate and trust Him for what was next. So we became full-time RVers with our boys, pleading with God for direction. We thought we were stepping out in obedience. We didn't know we were stepping into one of the hardest seasons of our lives. As months passed and our income plummeted, what had felt like an adventure began to feel like a freefall.

At first, the adventure masked the anxiety. We explored Colorado, Utah, Arizona. But as the decline deepened, the mask slipped. When the sun set, my mind returned to its frantic grasping.

I was desperate for peace. But I wouldn't receive it. Not yet.

As I journaled through those early morning spirals, a pattern emerged: I had built a checklist of conditions God needed to meet before I would accept His peace. I was holding peace hostage, barricading my heart behind demands.

First, I needed a home. I obsessed over real estate listings in every town we visited, searching for signs this might be where He was calling us. But God remained quiet.

Then I needed clarity about the business, the finances, the future. I needed to know how this story would end before I would let my heart rest.

From my lips, I said I trusted Him. But every morning I'd wake up anxious, refresh my email compulsively, scroll through listings. Trying to engineer my own rescue. I couldn't just wait on God.

But looking back, I see what I couldn't then: not one day did my family lack what we needed. God was faithful. Yet underneath my gratitude lived a deeper grief.

One morning, I finally stopped performing my prayers. I poured out my grief unfiltered.

"God, are You even watching? Do You see what I've lost? Or worse, do You not care?"

And then, finally, He spoke. Not audibly. Not dramatically. A gentle whisper that cut through every defense:

"Weslynn, I haven't taken anything from you."

Silence.

I wanted to argue. I had my list ready: the business, the security, the home, the future we'd planned. But something in His tone stopped me. Not harsh. Not dismissive. Just true.

And that's when it hit me: I was grieving the loss of things that were never mine to begin with. I'm a steward, not an owner. I had been clutching these gifts so tightly, demanding God guarantee their permanence before I would trust Him.

I saw it clearly: I wasn't as surrendered as I thought. I'd been running on self-manufactured peace, produced through control and contingency plans. Not the peace the Holy Spirit offers when we rest in Him.

I'd been trying to manufacture my own safety, when all along the Psalmist had it right: "You alone, Lord, make me dwell in safety" (Psalm 4:8 ESV).

And suddenly I understood. God wasn't withholding peace until I figured everything out. He'd been offering it all along. I was the one refusing to receive it, demanding He meet my conditions first, and insisting He check off my list.

I wasn't waiting on God's peace. His peace was waiting on me.

I wish I could say everything changed in that moment, but trust came in layers. Like laundry, there's always another load. Slowly, I broke free.

The first morning I didn't check my bank account felt like betrayal. But I did it anyway. And then the next day. Slowly, my mornings became conversations instead of audits.

I released my demands and learned to stop holding peace hostage. I had been denying myself the very gift He was offering, all because I needed guarantees. But that's not how His kingdom works. He's the King. I'm His daughter. Daughters don't need all the answers. They just need to trust their Father.

My peace couldn't hinge on knowing where we'd land or how this would end. It had to rest in trusting God, period. Trusting that He wasn't abandoning me, still with me, still working.

Peace isn't what I thought it was. It doesn't depend on having answers. It's available right now, in the middle of the mess. But I had to stop bracing for the next blow. Stop making endless backup plans. Stop chaining peace to my conditions.

I had to set it free.

These days, I watch the sunrise from a small farming town in Ohio, exactly where God called us. There are still things I'm waiting on, still mornings I choose trust over control.

But I don't wake up at 5 a.m. with tears anymore.

This morning, I watched the sky turn charcoal to gold, and I felt it. That peace I'd spent so long refusing. Not because everything is settled. Not because I have answers. But because I finally learned to receive what He'd been offering all along.

Peace isn't the absence of loss or perfect circumstances. It's knowing that even in the middle of the mess, I'm not alone. He's in control. And He's enough.

I knew it was my own mindset blocking peace, not God withholding it. But knowing and choosing are different things. For months, I'd been standing at the door, refusing to walk through.

I just had to choose it. Choose to receive the peace He'd been offering me all along.

And when I finally did, I realized: I wasn't setting myself free. I was setting peace free to do what it had been trying to do all along.

Weslynn Biggers is an ordained minister, coach, writer, and speaker living in central Ohio where she and her husband Brannon pastor their community. She's the creator of The Birthing Room, a mentorship community for women walking through seasons of becoming. Weslynn writes about the messy middle, where faith meets fear and peace waits to be received.

DROWNING IN PEACE

Morgan Blair

I could feel life pulling harder than I could keep up with. Everything I had worked so hard to hold steady was slipping beneath the surface, and I was desperate just to stay afloat.

Every change pulled me further off balance. Ordinary things in my life seemed to carry the weight of an anchor, sinking me deeper into my anxious mind. Things like my firstborn starting preschool: I was torn between the guilt of loving the quiet moments with my newborn and the joy of knowing my son was having fun there. I was also still trying to find my rhythm with two kids, always stressing about whether I was loving them equally or if one was left needing more of me. And then there was my business, quietly slipping out of focus, leaving me feeling like I'd failed both my clients and my family. Just as I was barely keeping my head above water, another wave hit.

"I think we should move" my husband said, "I think now is the best time to build and move back closer to family."

The words hit like a rogue wave against my chest. Although, that was always the plan to build and move back closer to family, it was too soon in my plan. We had poured so much love into our home, it felt like a dream was unraveling. I wrestled against the thoughts in my mind for weeks, fighting to keep up with the current around me, until one day I couldn't fight anymore.

My heart raced, as if it were trying to escape my chest. A bottomless pit formed in my stomach. Fear gripped me so tight, I couldn't breathe. My thoughts tumbled out of control, and it felt like my body was shutting down. Fear had become my compass, and anxiety took over.

Joy seemed to have disappeared from my life. I lived with apprehension, bracing for the next wave to drag me deeper into the sea of despair. Eventually the chaos gave way to emotional exhaustion, where a new kind of storm rose inside me. Where was God in all of this? Why wasn't He rescuing me? The silence made me wonder if He'd ever been near at all. Frustration boiled up inside me, and I started to feel angry with God.

Another day began, the heaviness of anxiety still sitting on my chest. Everything was changing so fast. There was a "for sale" sign in my front yard, another on my business, and even motherhood, the thing that once brought me the most joy, had become a heavy burden I didn't have the strength to carry. As the panic began to build within my chest, I ran to hide in the back of my closet, hoping not to be found. With tears streaming down my face, I cried out to God. This time, instead of asking God to take my anxiety away, I asked, "God, what are you teaching me through this?" As I sat there, finally letting go, in a place where I hoped to not be found, I found God.

Sitting there on my hands and knees, in full surrender, these words came to mind, "Come to me, all you who are weary and burdened, and I will give you rest" (Matthew 11:28). For so long, I had carried the weight of my world. All of my fears, my expectations, and the quiet ache of holding everything together for everyone, was lying on my shoulders. I was realizing peace had never come from my control, but from surrendering it all to Jesus. At that moment, I felt the heaviness begin to lift from my chest, and the sun began to peek through the clouds in my mind. As the Lord wrapped His arms around me, I felt His gentle reminder that peace is not the absence of hardships, but trusting Him through them.

As I started trusting God through my storm, I thought of the night Jesus called Peter onto the waves. I envisioned him taking that first step off the boat, trembling with fear, both eyes locked on Jesus. When doubt hit, fear stole his focus and the sea rose up to swallow him. I saw myself there with Peter. I had taken my eyes off Jesus too: sinking beneath the weight of my own fears, drowning in the waters of doubt, change, and distraction. Like Peter, I cried out to Jesus for help, and just as He reached for Peter's hand, I felt Him graciously reach for mine.

His presence did not remove the storm, but it quieted the one inside me. That's where I found the peace Jesus promised: not a peace that erases the waves, but one that holds me steady upon them. My faith no longer depends on calm seas, but it rests on the One who walks upon them.

Morgan Blair, a wife and mom of three, is following her calling to help others discover a deeper, more meaningful relationship with Jesus. Through her writing and voice, she encourages faith that goes beyond routine. Learn more about Morgan at www.blairfaithproject.com.

THERE IS PEACE IN THE KNOWING

Lainey Forde Bradley

On my forty-ninth birthday I did not want to live. Three days earlier, my husband, Phillip, was killed instantly in a tragic car accident on a familiar route home from work. A man dedicated to his faith, family, and career was suddenly gone. Any feeling of peace or tranquility was absent from my mind, body, and soul. From the moment a sheriff's officer told me, "Your husband didn't make it," and for months after, I was crushed by the weight of despair. My chest ached, as though my heart had been torn from it. Each throbbing panic attack dimmed my vision and took my breath away. My mind scrambled to recall our final conversations and cling to our last memories. I went through the motions of eating what I could tolerate, planning his memorial, and facing painful administrative tasks. My broken heart wasn't in any of it. I didn't want to live in a world where Phillip would no longer be.

In my devastation and deep sorrow, the feeling of peace was elusive. However, I realized there is peace found in knowing of God's ability to both welcome a loved one into His heavenly realm and also remain a constant presence with those who must survive in the wake of crushing loss. My awareness of the difference between feeling peace and knowing peace took many months of praying and wrestling with God.

At first, the absence of peace in my body and soul not only weakened my will to keep going but also eroded my relationship with God. I asked Him, "Why have You abandoned the family we have built over twenty-five years? Why has this happened to us, a couple who kept our faith a priority? Why did this happen to a man with so much purpose as a dad, husband, son, and a nurse with a strong calling to his career? Why, Lord?"

Although God felt distant in my suffering, I never questioned whether my husband was safe in the hands of our Heavenly Father. From the moment I was told the first details of the severe impact Phillip faced and could not endure, I envisioned God scooping him up immediately and without suffering. But, this assurance that God had mercifully rescued him from a devastating collision did not translate to a feeling of peace in my heart.

My desire to live was a flicker rather than a steady light. But through the loved ones who cared for us, God was present in our pain. I was unable to see Him fully, but I now know He had not abandoned us. Two occasions of encouragement, in particular, became anchoring threads I wove through my daily battles with sadness, doubt, and brokenness.

The first was a card from my sister reminding me to breathe and find strength from the truth that Phillip was safely in heaven and in my heart. The card referenced the prophetic words of Micah 5:4–5: "He will stand and shepherd his flock in the strength of the Lord, in the majesty of the name of the Lord his God. And they will live securely, for then his greatness will reach to the ends of the earth. And he will be their peace . . . ." Micah was speaking of Jesus's eventual birth and life on earth, sacrificially leading all those who followed him to eternal life. When I remembered "he will be their peace," I began to understand that God was not only sovereign over my husband's life but also over mine (Micah 5:5). He had never forsaken us, but instead He was ever-present.

My second moment of clarity occurred eight months after Phillip's death, on our twenty-sixth wedding anniversary. A flower delivery and message arrived from our daughter, Julia. She knew her dad would have brought flowers to me, and her remembrance eased my heartache. The card attached to the flowers read: "You are loved by me, Will (our son), and Dad from heaven! Most importantly, you're loved by our Heavenly Father." Her message ended with 2 Corinthians 4:18, in which the apostle Paul wrote, "So we fix our eyes not on what is seen, but on what is unseen, since what is seen is temporary, but what is unseen is eternal."

My daughter's words took my breath away, because they sounded exactly like something Phillip would have said. Through tears, I saw a part of his legacy already living on: the faith and confidence in God he'd always freely shared was now reflected in her words. The scripture revived an assurance in me: God came to earth as Jesus Christ to defeat death and secure our place in the kingdom of heaven, where we will join Him when it is our time. I had a revelation: Phillip was in the unseen realm of heaven; I was only seeing an earthly scene of hopelessness and depression. I hadn't allowed God to lovingly shift my eyes to the unseen and the promise of eternal life my husband was experiencing. I needed to grasp the truth that God will deliver the same promise to me, but only He knows when.

If you are grieving a significant person's death, living with their absence can feel like trudging through a deep valley, untethered from any safety ropes to pull you from the depths. Feeling peace can seem impossible, as you struggle to redefine your identity and make sense of "why" questions which may never have earthly answers. But an assurance of God's steadfast presence and eternal promises has rooted deeper in my soul, even when peace as a feeling hasn't prevailed over my anxiety or loneliness. By remembering the abundant peace of God in the unseen and how Jesus made it possible, those who have lost a loved one can find strength to keep living in their memory. There is peace in the knowing that God's sovereignty over your loved one's life and death applies to yours, too.

LAINEY FORDE BRADLEY

Lainey Forde Bradley is a mother of two young adults, sister, aunt, high school educator, author, and widows ministry volunteer. She leans on her love of writing to process grief following tragedy. Lainey and her beloved pets live north of Atlanta, and you can follow her on Facebook or Instagram.

SINGING IN THE RAIN

Angela Buckland

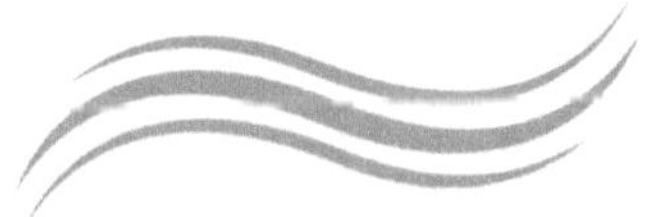

Fifteen minutes before the ceremony, the Georgia sky split wide open.

We'd spent over a year planning the perfect day: our firstborn's dream wedding in early June, flowers in full bloom, and late afternoon sunlight filtering through the trees. The weather had been flawless all day. As loved ones began to arrive, ominous clouds like uninvited guests threatened to ruin our plans. Then it started raining in buckets.

Everyone scrambled for cover. Amid the chaos, I looked over and saw the bride's lip begin to quiver, and her eyes welled with tears. Her bouquet trembled in her hands, her chest rising and falling, breath growing shallow as she watched her wedding hopes dashed right before her eyes. I recognized the signs immediately: a panic attack was setting in. After months of preparation, everything was about to fall apart.

Well-intentioned coordinators and one very nervous mother-of-the-bride huddled around her, asking what she wanted to do. Should we delay? Move inside? Wait it out? In that moment, I saw my own anxiety reflected back: the frantic need to fix, control, problem-solve. Our analytical minds grasped for solutions and logistics.

But then, in a holy hush, she whispered words no one expected to hear: "Can we worship?"

We stopped, gaping at one another, stunned by the maturity and the vulnerability of her response. The worship leader picked up his guitar, and everyone lifted their voices in gratitude.

Under that covered porch, with rain drumming on the roof and thunder rumbling in the background like a distant drumbeat, our timid voices sang in unison, swelling and steadying with each refrain. The bride led us that day, praising God for His goodness, and one by one, the voices of the bridesmaids and groomsmen all joined in. My own voice cracked on the second verse, but I kept singing through the tightness in my throat. As her mother, I'd never been prouder.

The bouquet stopped shaking in her hands.

The rain surrounded us like a curtain, a heavenly veil isolating our small gathering from the rest of the world. The whole mood shifted, and tranquility replaced panic. The bride's tense shoulders began to drop. Her breathing slowed and deepened. We sang through tears and raindrops, our voices building and blending in with the storm.

I felt the knot in my own chest release with each refrain. Water dripped from the porch eaves. The scent of rain mixed with the sweetness of grass and earthy red clay. Thunder rumbled in the background, but grew distant with each verse, more like accompaniment, less like a threat.

When we finished singing, the rest that followed was different from the stunned silence of moments before. This silence held peace and a sense of completion, not because the storm had stopped, but because we had surrendered and invited Jesus into it.

We were not the first to find Jesus' peace in the middle of a storm. In Luke 8:22-25, His disciples faced a fierce gale that filled their boat with water and put even seasoned fishermen in danger. Scripture doesn't gloss over this: they were in real danger. Their fear was legitimate.

They woke Jesus, crying, "Master, Master, we're going to drown!" (Luke 8:24).

Jesus calmed the storm first, then asked them: "Where is your faith?" (Luke 8:25).

Rather than an accusation, Jesus offers an invitation: Where is your faith? In the weather changing? In your ability to bail water fast enough? Or in Me?

I'm no stranger to chasing peace in all the wrong places. I've scrolled to numb myself, over-functioned to feel in control, and sought validation from others to feel secure. That rainy afternoon, my daughter showed me a different way. When she asked, "Can we worship?" she wasn't asking for the storm to stop. She chose to run to Jesus while it raged around her.

The rain continued, and they exchanged vows that day under umbrellas, surrounded by mud puddles and laughter. What could have been a disaster is now a sacred memory of the most beautiful day. A summer downpour stripped away our illusion of control, leaving what mattered most: worship, love, and Jesus' abiding presence that never abandons us.

In John 14:27, Jesus says, "Peace I leave with you; my peace I give you. I do not give to you as the world gives. Do not let your hearts be troubled and do not be afraid." True peace isn't something we manufacture through striving or control. It's found in a Person. It comes when we surrender to the One who commands wind and waves with a single word.

Jesus promised, "In this world you will have trouble" (John 16:33). The question isn't whether we'll face storms. We will. The question is: where will our faith be when they come?

On that unforgettable day, peace came when we stopped, when we turned to Him and worshiped. And He is here with you today, in whatever storm you face, waiting and ready to be your peace when you whisper, "Can we worship?"

ANGELA BUCKLAND

 Wife to Ren and mom to four grown kids, Angela Buckland knows the joy and challenge of juggling faith, family, and calling. She serves as a Discipleship Director at Bethlehem Church while pursuing a Master of Divinity. She loves creating spaces for women to meet Jesus, find encouragement, and grow together. http:// angelabuckland.com

STICKS AND STONES:

FINDING PEACE THAT
WORDS CANNOT STEAL

Shannon M. Carducci

One of the biggest lies I believed growing up was "sticks and stones may break my bones, but words will never hurt." Why is it, then, that I remember insults directed at me from bullies in elementary school that still sting? And even today, words have caused some of the deepest hurts in my life. The emotional pain from words can create chaos and steal inner peace. But too often, I let the sting of hurtful words penetrate my heart and leave me feeling empty, lost, and crushed. I'm learning that true peace must come from within, not from what others say, though that lesson cost me plenty to learn. Although I've allowed words to steal my peace more times than I'd like to admit, I know Christ can offer me peace that transcends any circumstance!

I've been struggling lately with someone in my life who unleashed on me with an unwarranted rant filled with hateful words, lies, and accusations. The sting of those words and their constant echo in my head left me desolate. I stayed trapped in anger, sadness, and disbelief for far too long. I struggled to find peace as those callous words cycled endlessly through my mind, wrenching my heart. In Proverbs 18:21, we see clearly how words have the power to bring us encouragement, but also deep pain: "The tongue has the power of life and death . . . " There was nothing life-giving in the words hurled at me.

My experience isn't unique. In any conflict between people, I'm confident that hurtful words played a role. Sadly, the most significant pain often comes from someone close to us. So, what do you do with that pain? How do you find peace when words left wounds that time hasn't healed? Scripture is filled with passages showing how Jesus is the source of and giver of peace! One that I find helpful as I cry out for healing from the hurt is Psalm 34:18: "The Lord is close to the brokenhearted and saves those who are crushed in spirit." There are days when all I can do is recite that verse over and over and trust that it is true.

My struggle for peace has exposed a conflict within me: the difference between worldly peace and God's peace. For so long, I believed peace meant everything going right: people treating me well, circumstances working in my favor. Even if those words were spoken, even if they hurt, my identity and worth aren't determined by them. That truth is found in John 14:27: "Peace I leave with you; my peace I give you. I do not give to you as the world gives . . ." That's the kind of peace I need in my life!

Just because I know the truth, that Jesus has given me the gift of peace through the Holy Spirit and His

Word, doesn't mean it's not an ongoing struggle. The scars left and the emotional toll I've experienced have made it necessary to fight to keep my peace.

So how do I fight? Each morning, before my feet even hit the floor, I ask God to fill me with the fruit of His Spirit: love, joy, peace, patience, kindness, goodness, faithfulness, gentleness, and self-control (Galatians 5:22-23). That practice has become my lifeline, a reminder that these gifts are available to me even on the hardest days. Beyond that, worship music is another lifeline for me. God's words are strewn throughout worship music and amplified in my heart. It's a beautiful and freeing thing to sing and praise God, allowing the truths of His love to heal my brokenness.

Personal struggles like these have shown me I need to break the family cycle of hurt I've witnessed. Hurt people hurt people. I've seen it, felt it. And I refuse to be that person. I want my words to bring life, to inspire and encourage, not to crush and discourage. I'm responsible for my own healing. That means protecting myself from further emotional abuse while choosing to create peace, not chaos.

Yes, I'm reclaiming the truth the childhood rhyme denied: words DO hurt. But I'm also embracing a greater truth: that God's peace is stronger! Through that peace, I've found forgiveness for the one who wounded me and for myself for the bitterness I've carried. This frees me to live in the peace Christ offers, regardless of what others say.

It's been quite a journey from being shattered by words to resting in God's truth. As I reflect on that painful day and see how much healing has come, I'm reminded: I can choose peace, offer grace, and use my words to heal rather than harm. Not because I've arrived, but because I'm learning that His peace really is enough. Even on the mornings when it doesn't feel like enough, it is.

Shannon M. Carducci is a ministry leader and writer who loves Jesus, her family, and discovering new places. Married nearly 30 years with 5 grown kids and 7 grandkids, she's embracing her second act as an empty-nester with joy and gratitude. Connect with her on Instagram @gracecitygirl.

FINDING PEACE IN THE MIDDLE OF A BREAKDOWN

Gina Colburn

I did not expect peace to come through a breakdown. Yet in the fall of 2018, somewhere between a solo drive to Washington, D.C. and a surrendering moment in a hotel room, I began to find myself again. Or maybe for the first time.

For decades I had been a people-pleasing, do-more, always-on-call kind of woman. My identity shifted with every label I thought fit me: leader, pastor, mother, wife, sister, friend. I worked 70-hour workweeks, cooked homemade meals like Martha Stewart, and answered every ding from my phone around the clock. Then I wondered why I felt so empty. Looking back, I can see how easily I had started listening to lies around me. The loudest lie said, "If I slow down or delegate, I can and will be replaced." I allowed it without thinking. I didn't realize it then, but September would be the beginning of a shift toward healing and hope.

The weight of it all felt crushing. Leading a church bursting at the seams, navigating staff conflict that kept me up at night, holding my family together through upheaval, all while my own expectations whispered that a better leader would make it look easy. Even the small things, like a missed call or an overflowing trash can, would throw me over the edge. Each one was a reminder that I was not enough. For years, I feared I was never quite enough, that God was tired of me, frustrated with me, or over me. Yet, Jesus' pursuit of me with his unending grace met me right where I was. But on that drive to D.C., I felt His presence differently. He still loved me. He still offered lifelines in the middle of my mess.

When I arrived in D.C., the awareness of God's presence followed me as I wandered around the museums. As I walked through the Museum of the Bible, I felt anchored in history. I watched a film on the New Testament. I stood before fragments of ancient scrolls. I paused at the exhibit of Billy Graham, a man God used to lead millions to Jesus. In the background, one of his sermons echoed alongside the familiar strains of an altar-call hymn. I found myself wondering: Who might be the next Billy Graham? Could God use someone like me: broken, exhausted, barely holding on?

Later, at the Holocaust Museum, I was handed a card with the name of Tchiya Perlmutter, a real woman who died at the hands of the Nazis. In one room, thousands of worn shoes filled a display. This room always arrests me. Rows of shoes that once carried lives, steps, and stories now stand silent. They belonged to people who never knew where their final footsteps would lead.

Standing in the room of shoes, I felt the weight of lives cut short and the reality of this one life I have here. My head spun as I moved from the history of the Bible to the horror of the Holocaust, from the Jewish people's sacred texts to their mass persecution. Somehow, amid the overwhelm, a question surfaced: How am I participating in what God is doing all around me and what am I holding on to that I need to release?

The question followed me to the hotel where I had planned to take a nap. Instead, I felt prompted to open my Bible to Jeremiah 15:18-22, a passage that reminds me that when we return to God, He will heal our wounds. I read it aloud and prayed: for my family, for my church, and, strangely, for myself. It felt unusual to pray boldly that God might use me and heal me, yet the words poured out. Then came stillness.

In that quiet, I sensed Jesus telling me to kneel before Him. At first, I hesitated, but I obeyed. Kneeling turned to face-down surrender on the floor of that D.C. hotel room, my forehead pressed against the rough carpet, which will forever be a sacred place of remembrance for me.

I saw Jesus' hands: nail-pierced, bruised. His gentle voice said, "Look at my hands. Look upon my face." I heard Him telling me He had forgiven everything I had done and would do. He said because of Him, I was enough. The chains of my past and the fears of my future were nailed to the cross. He could handle every battle I was facing personally and in leading a church. Tears flowed as His presence became tangible. He confirmed that my call was right where I was; my task was to speak boldly and write faithfully. This was how I would participate in what He was doing. I realized afresh that Jesus was a real, breathing person who came to save me, not only for eternity but this one life I have right now.

Rising from the floor, I knew that circumstances had not changed, but I had. My heart didn't feel like it was going to beat out of my chest. The ugly voices were silent. It was as if peace seeped into the cracks of my soul. Not the kind of peace that comes from a clear schedule or a quiet house, but the deep, steady peace that holds you steady when everything around you feels chaotic. I began to find rest and sleep again: real sleep, the kind that refreshes and attunes the heart to Jesus.

Something new was alive in me. Sometimes faithfulness means knowing when to let go of the expectation that I had to be perfect, of the fear that I'd be replaced if I rested, of roles within the church that weren't mine to carry. I learned that participating in God's work doesn't mean saying yes to everything. It means saying yes to the right things.

Peace didn't come because I pieced my life together. It came because, in surrender, I met the One who had been holding it all along.

Gina Colburn is a writer, speaker, and storyteller who helps others find meaning in their everyday lives through faith and reflection. She is the creator of "Gina's Table" and lives in Kansas with her husband, Jason, their four children, and growing family.

FOR WHEN
YOU CAN'T SLEEP

Kayla M. Cook

"In peace I will both lie down and sleep; for you alone, O LORD, make me dwell in safety."

Psalm 4:8 (ESV)

My eyes flew open in the dark. My pounding heart woke me up from a dead sleep, with every heartbeat screaming, *get up, get up, GET UP.*

It was 5:28 a.m., and I was on vacation.

Having just been jarred awake, my eyes were slowly adjusting to the dark room, but my brain was running full speed ahead, trying to figure out why I had been shaken awake so suddenly.

As my eyes continued to adjust, I scanned the room for the apparent danger my body and brain were screaming about. I felt the soft and cool sheets on a comfy bed in a beautiful hotel room, "Happy Anniversary!" card on the nightstand. My excellent husband was sleeping soundly and our suitcases sat packed in the corner, ready for an on-time flight home to our daughter.

With nothing I could see making any sense, *Why is my heart pounding?* became the question I asked myself over and over, trying to identify the source of this unwelcome wake up. My body recognized it before my mind did: after being able to disconnect and get away, I was heading back into the pressure of feeling like I'm not enough for my life.

It was an intense season for our family. Intense does not always mean bad. In our case, it meant productive work, a full schedule, leading in our church, and being involved in our daughter's school. Life was full and we were grateful, but we were also tired from doing it all with minimal support, and in some cases, intense does mean bad. Our friends and family were themselves navigating so much grief, chronic illness, cancer, caregiving, and more.

We were doing our best to love and support one another in the midst of it all, but I always felt like I was coming up short. A hard-fought, years-long battle with anxiety returned during this time, and yet, I felt like I should have been handling it better. We had been through much harder, much worse, and made it. Nothing I did felt good enough, and I carried a lot of guilt and shame for being stressed, for wishing things were different.

Why was my body choosing now, at the peaceful end of a sweet getaway, to overreact?

My heart continued pounding as I tiptoed across the room. I filled a glass with cold water, taking small sips and breathing deeply between each one, hoping for some relief. As I began to slow my breathing and hope my pulse would match that pace, I remembered a previous season of anxiety.

I hoped to be comforted by this memory, thinking that knowing I had made it through before would encourage me that I would make it through again. Instead, it made me sad, mad, and even more anxious. I had the benefit of hindsight, but I had the scars, too. The dread settled over me with each thought of being back here in the dark spiral of anxiety, of how tough this battle would be, and not knowing how long it would last.

Above the noise in my brain and the pounding in my heart, a verse I once cherished rose to the surface of my mind. Over days and weeks and months I had previously spent in the dark, burdened by anxiety and unable to sleep, I would repeat this verse until sleep finally came: "I will lie down in peace and sleep, for you, alone, O LORD, make me dwell in safety (Psalm 4:8 ESV).

Peace is a requirement for sleep. It's why we invest in things like blackout curtains, pillows of our desired firmness or softness, sleep masks, white noise machines. It's why we turn down our thermostats and want blankets at a just-right weight.

Those things are good and helpful, but where does the peace to sleep really come from?

Peace comes from knowing we can sleep because God alone makes us dwell in safety.

Peace comes from knowing rest is a gift from the Lord for the people He loves (Psalm 127:2 ESV).

Peace comes from knowing the One who calms every storm, the ones on the water and the ones in our hearts.

I don't know what's keeping you up at night, but I know the One who knows, and we can take heart and live in His peace because He has overcome the world.

I never went back to sleep that morning, but that night, I was able to get some rest. Even now, some nights are good, and some are not, and I'm learning to embrace the waves that come with being human. Even so, on the nights when I find myself staring at the ceiling, I go back to what I know to be true: "In peace I will both lie down and sleep; for you alone, O LORD, make me dwell in safety" (Psalm 4:8 ESV).

There is peace for you, even here, enough peace to sleep.

Kayla M. Cook is a wife, mom, author, speaker, and the host of The Bitter & the Sweet podcast. With candor, humor, and a 'what you see is what you get' approach, Kayla points out God's faithfulness in her stories to help you see His faithfulness in yours.

PEACE HELD ME

Megan Davis

y shoulders slumped, my head bowed, and my whole body melted as I said, "Okay, Jesus, okay. I trust you." Hot tears streamed from my eyes, stinging with heartache and regret and shame and helplessness. I could not go back and change what had been done.

I hadn't slept a full night in almost 2 years. I'd fall asleep but then be jolted awake, heart pounding, mind racing, flooded with regret. The questions bullied me daily. How could I be this stupid? Why had I trusted them? If only I could take that one decision back! How will I ever recover from this?

Fifty pounds heavier, I barely recognized myself. Every joint ached. My hands cramped around my coffee mug. The rheumatologist said the word: fibromyalgia. He pleaded with me to deal with my grief and self-blame to calm my system so that I could heal. The Lord had been pleading with me too. For months during my morning times with him on my deck, he pressed me to trust him. I couldn't do it, I couldn't stop fighting! I had to claw my way out of the nightmare my one decision had made of my life.

How did I get here?

Eighteen months earlier, I found myself in a family court custody case. I never could have imagined the decisions that would be made there. Ultimately I lost the right to determine my daughter's primary residence. Having to watch her move a thousand miles away was crushing.

During that difficult season, the Lord began showing me visions of parents from scripture placing their children in God's hands. They had to trust Him to shield, carry, guide their children when they were helpless to do so themselves.

I was ready to sell my house to pay lawyers and get things back to the way they were. With a heart overwhelmed with a mothers love I would have gladly given up everything to hear her down the hall laughing and playing make believe with her brother. I was not going to let my child go. No. Hard stop. I wanted the Lord to orchestrate a miraculous restoration!

I was begging Him!

But I felt like He was refusing.

The Lord asked: "Can you trust me like these parents did?"

Through tears, snot, and white-hot rage, I answered: "I don't know!"

One of the parents He had shown me was Mary, the mother of Jesus, as Michelangelo portrayed her in 'La Pietà'—holding her son's lifeless body. I had to look away.

I couldn't stop seeing myself in her grief. Her open palm speaks: "May it happen to me as you have said" (Luke 1:38 CSB). But she also seems to plead, as I was doing, asking God to reach down, show his power, and DO SOMETHING! Please.

Day after day, the Lord challenged me to let go and trust him with one of my most precious gifts (only in 4th grade at the time). Morning after morning I said "No! There's got to be another way! Show me your love by undoing this horrible thing!"

As the days turned into months, I didn't sleep. I gained weight. My body was in pain literally from head to toe. The legal bills mounted and the decisions being made by court "professionals" were stunning and terrible. I clawed and raged at the devil and begged the Lord. I sought advice from everyone who would listen and seemed to have been through a similar nightmare.

Finally, one morning in the cool of spring, wrapped in my blanket and sipping my coffee, I broke. I had come to the end of myself. I crumpled in my chair and as I melted in sadness I whimpered, "Okay, Jesus, I will trust You to take care of her. You have walked me through two miscarriages, through divorce, through poverty, through chronic illness and I trust that You have heard my cries and You will again be found trustworthy with this awful situation too."

That night I slept for the first time in almost two years.

Something shifted in my body. The knot in my stomach unclenched. My shoulders dropped. For the first time in months, I took a full breath without my chest feeling wrapped in barbed wire.

It made no sense. Nothing about my situation had changed. My child was still gone. I had lost the legal battle. But I slept. Eight hours. Dreamless. When I woke, the panic wasn't there.

I can't tie this up with a bow. There's no moment when everything was fixed. Almost 8 years later, she still doesn't live with me. But what I can offer you is hope. In your worst decisions. In life-altering regret. In debilitating shame. Jesus is there, holding you, calming you. Just like He did for me.

Sleep can be an act of faith. It is evidence of peace, trust, and knowing who holds us in the storm. Jesus, in the boat, slept in the storm too, not because the storm wasn't violently shaking everything around Him, but because He trusted the one who held Him in the midst of it.

In order to sleep I had to surrender. I had to unclench my grip on control of the situation. I had to admit I couldn't burn it down and make it right again.

I asked myself back then, "How can I ever recover from this?"

Recovery isn't what I thought. It's not fixing what broke. It's learning to sleep in the storm. Trusting Jesus when I can't understand why He's allowing the storm to continue.

I'm recovering, my friend. Right now. Tonight. I have peace in my body and in my mind because I have chosen to surrender control, even of my worst decisions, to the Prince of Peace.

And when you're ready to stop clawing and thrashing and instead, trust.

He will hold and calm you too.

Megan Davis is a life coach, speaker, and author who helps women heal from narcissistic abuse. Blending faith, practical wisdom, and lived experience, she guides women to reclaim identity, restore peace, and rise with courage. Her work empowers them to build lives rooted in wholeness, freedom, and God-led purpose.

THE BEAUTIFUL ACHE OF MOTHERHOOD

Charlotte P. Edwards

There's a sound no mother ever forgets: the crack in her child's voice when they're hurting.

Three weeks after I dropped my son off at military college, I picked up the phone and heard his voice crack. He was exhausted, miserable, homesick. "Mom, I can't do this. I need to come home."

I sank onto the edge of my bed, phone pressed to my ear, and my heart broke. My mom-heart screamed: Go get him. End this. Bring him home.

But another voice, quieter, steadier, cut through: *Charlotte, you didn't raise him to be comfortable. You raised him to be strong. Don't undo that now.* Deep down, I knew this wasn't a season for me to swoop in and rescue. This was the stretching: the holy discomfort that grows a boy into a man. If he leaves now, he'll wonder for the rest of his life if he could have made it.

God didn't place me here to shield him from every storm. God placed me here to pray him through it, to trust that God was with him, even when I couldn't be.

I wish I could say that prayer solved everything. It didn't.

When he finally got his phone back, I was relieved. I was able to talk to him again. But it became both a blessing and a curse. His name lit up my screen at all hours, some texts making my heart swell over an accomplishment, others creating instant anxiety. I'd have to pause before opening them, asking myself: *Am I in the mental space to read this right now? Or should I wait?*

I knew this road would be harder for him than the typical college experience. But I didn't anticipate the emotional roller coaster it would be for me. Every notification. Every call. Every silence.

Meanwhile, my social media was filled with other parents posting about football games and parents' weekends, their kids smiling in group photos. And my son was grinding through something that would break most people.

The weight of that contrast sat with me everywhere. At work, when a friend asked, "How's your son doing at school?" I smiled and said, "He's adjusting." What I didn't say: "He's miserable. He wants to quit. And I won't let him."

There were days I wanted to drive there and pull him out myself. Days I questioned everything. Was I being strong or just cruel? Was this character-building or was I letting him suffer needlessly?

One of those nights, around 2 a.m., a text came in: "I don't think I can do another day of this." I sat up in bed, phone glowing in the dark. My fingers started moving before I'd even fully processed what he texted. I sent him a paragraph about how strong he was. Then another about all the reasons this would be worth it. Then Scripture. Then encouragement. Then a pep talk that would've rallied a football team.

Six messages. Six desperate attempts to be enough.

He didn't respond. I lay there in the dark, phone clutched in my hand, refreshing the screen for hours. By morning, he still hadn't replied. When he finally texted all he said was: "Thanks, Mom." While I'd spent seven hours in a spiral of anxiety, he'd been fine. He needed a sounding board. I'd given him a megaphone.

I kept trying to be both. Another night, another phone call. I said everything I could think of. When we hung up, I was exhausted, not from talking, but from the weight of trying to hold us both up. I got on my knees, hands open, and whispered the only words I had left:

"Lord, he's Yours. You love him more than I ever could. You see him right now in his struggle. Be his peace when I cannot."

That's where peace became my only lifeline: not peace that meant everything was fine, but peace born from seeing this differently.

A few days later, I was scrolling on social media when one post stopped me. A friend had shared something about "bird launchers" instead of "empty nesters."

Bird launcher.

I exhaled. I wasn't an empty nester watching my son leave. I was a bird launcher watching him fly. Empty meant I'd lost something. Launcher meant I'd given something. One felt like loss. The other felt like purpose.

The ache didn't disappear. But it felt lighter somehow.

One morning, I was getting ready for work when a text came in from him. The old me would have opened it immediately, heart racing, bracing for crisis. This time, I paused. Set the phone down. Finished my makeup. I drove to work. And when I finally checked my phone two hours later, it was just a text saying he'd nailed PT that morning. I'd been so sure he needed me to respond immediately. But he didn't need me hovering. He just needed me believing he could handle it.

And slowly, over the weeks that followed, I learned a new rhythm. When he called struggling, I'd take a breath before responding. When texts came in at difficult moments, I'd wait until I could actually be present. I practiced saying less and trusting more. Some days I still wanted to fix everything. But more and more, I was learning to just witness—to be the sounding board he needed, not the megaphone I'd been.

Philippians 4:7 promises this: "And the peace of God, which surpasses all understanding, will guard your hearts and your minds in Christ Jesus" (ESV). I'd read that verse a hundred times. But I'd never lived it until now: in the breath I took before responding, in the phone I didn't check immediately, in the silence I learned to sit with instead of filling with solutions.

Several weeks later, my phone rang again. I steadied myself for another storm. But this time, when I answered, his voice carried new strength. Clearer. Steadier.

"Mom," he said, "whatever happens, don't let me quit. I know there are going to be days when all I want to do is quit. But please, help me remember why I'm here."

When we hung up, I sank into the quiet of my kitchen and wept. But these were different tears.

He was going to be okay.

And somewhere along the way, I'd learned to be okay with not being the one to make him okay.

That's the peace I'd been praying for without realizing it. The peace of surrender: the kind that comes when you finally unclench your fists and let God be God.

I still hear it sometimes—that crack in his voice when things get hard. And my heart still aches.

But I don't carry him anymore. God does.

He flies. I pray. God holds us both.

That's not emptiness. That's peace.

Charlotte P. Edwards is a nurse, coach, speaker, and writer who helps women find faith and purpose when life shifts. Shaped by her years in the NICU and her own unraveling seasons, she learned surrender is strength. She lives in Charleston, SC, and loves traveling, time with her family, and her two golden retrievers. Connect at www.charlottepedwards.com.

ANCHORED IN PEACE

Deborah France

We enter seasons of rushing waters, howling winds, and crashing waves, and it feels like everything is falling apart. These storms are where we have a choice: seek God or allow the world to pull us under. We sit in our story and nothing makes sense. Chaos and uncertainty swirl around, and peace feels like a faraway land we'll never set foot on.

This distant land tempts us to pull the blanket over our heads and hide from the world. But if you are anything like me, you don't hide. You convince yourself you can fix everything. I constantly created contingency plans for every situation. Full lists were my love language, and if I didn't have enough to do, I made sure to take on everyone else's world as well. These choices led to deeper disappointments and drew me further from God. When going through these stormy seasons, we can begin to wonder if peace is possible, or if it's only for people with less messy lives.

I know this struggle intimately. These past few years have brought more change than I could have anticipated. I remarried, blended a family, moved an hour away, bought a new home, left my ministry job, attended a new church, and enrolled my kids in new schools. Navigating so many life-altering circumstances has magnified my struggles and left my world unsettled. I have found myself face-to-face with crippling fear and anxiety, rooted in the weight of uncertainty.

Through these changes, I was changing. God was refining me, reshaping my heart, revealing His work, and showing me who was no longer meant to walk beside me. I had to find ways to quiet my uneasy soul. I realized that asking for help was not a weakness but a superpower. Therapy and wise counsel helped me wrestle with questions like, "What am I doing wrong? Why am I losing relationships? Why am I always burned out?" I learned it wasn't what I was doing wrong, it was my resistance to stillness and my inability to rest in the turbulence. My harsh reality sank in: I needed to be more intentional with my quiet time and make room for God in my everyday life.

As an extrovert, I filled every space of my life with noise and people to avoid confronting the deeper reason why peace felt like a fairy tale. The controlling, unrealistic expectations, overextending myself, overfunctioning, and my own inability to face the chaos within were a perfect recipe to have no space for peace to be in my days. My calendar had become a rainbow of responsibilities: four colors for each child, two for my husband and me, and one more for our endless medical appointments. Whenever I saw an open space, I started texting people, "Do you want to grab a coffee? Do you want to go to lunch?" I avoided stillness in order to avoid confronting my own discomforts.

But God had other plans. The most surprising, and painful, was losing friends I believed would be with me for a lifetime. I didn't recognize it at the time but God was carving out space in my life. Quiet space. Sacred space. Uncomfortable space. I had to make a choice: fill it again with comfortable unhealthy noise, or trust Him? I chose to trust Him.

It was time to be more intentional: silencing my phone and filling the room with instrumental worship music. Leaning into flickering candlelight, I breathed in calming aromas and allowed my walls to come down. God finally had the space to calm my spirit. There was no perfect recipe for what to do or how to do it. I learned to simply be, to be still and know that He would meet me there. I cried out to the Lord, jotting down prayers for people and situations, and simply listening for God to speak to my heart. These moments revealed my truth: the worn path I had been walking was no longer the one God intended for my life.

In the middle of my refining process, I learned peace would never come from changing my circumstances. It was found in my willingness to allow God to show me uncomfortable truths about myself. I realized that my need for control spoke louder than my trust in Him. Whenever things felt unsteady, I would try to artificially manufacture comfort that only God could provide.

Peace isn't found in the absence of chaos. It's found in the presence of God right in the eye of the storm. I could no longer overextend myself and believe everything would be made right. I couldn't chase friendships to find my worth, or seek peace through endless activity. I couldn't strive for significance and expect wholeness to follow. And I most certainly could not keep walking paths God never intended for me and believe things would somehow work out.

Something shifts when we release our need for everything to be made right. The waters may remain rough and dry land may be nowhere in sight, but I have learned it is in those seasons that God does His best work. We rarely see it in the middle of the storm, but when we choose to be still and make room for Him, we experience peace beyond anything we could have imagined.

Let peace be the anchor that steadies you through life's fiercest storms. Peace is not a destination but a way of living that grows in God's presence. Spend time with Him. Allow Him to reveal the deeper parts of yourself that need healing, and be willing to conquer whatever He shows you. My hope is that you, too, are journeying toward deeper peace, unshakeable hope, and joy that comes from trusting God. The winds may continue to howl and the waves continue to crash, but peace with Him will always give you a solid ground to stand on. Peace be with you, my friend, all your days.

Deborah France is a Yankee turned Southern writer, speaker, minister, and coach who tackles the messy stuff—faith, family, feelings—with brutal honesty and lots of love. Blended family survivor, truth-teller, and hope enthusiast. She's rewriting the faith playbook one uncomfortable conversation at a time. Find her at www.deborahfrance.com

THANK GOD FOR MY THIGHS:

MY JOURNEY TO FINDING
PEACE WITH MY BODY

Jordan Horvath

My longest fight has been with the image I see in the mirror.

For as long as I can remember, my body and I have been in conflict. Even as a young girl, I remember knowing there was a body standard, and for some reason, I wasn't meeting it. It wasn't just that I felt awkward. Certainly having acne, teeth in dire need of braces, and hair that was straight-ish didn't help, but it went much deeper. My interests were ballet, cheerleading, and beauty pageants, which were definitely not activities for someone called a "good eater" (I think it was meant as a compliment?).

From an early age, it felt like there was only one firm conclusion: God must have made a mistake.

This narrative seemed to be confirmed again and again throughout middle school. I couldn't make the cheerleading squad, no matter how hard I tried. I also remember on football game days, boys would give their jerseys to a girl to wear at school. I was never asked to wear a jersey, and as much as I want to believe it didn't impact me, I can still feel the pain of rejection. There were girls who were good enough, thin enough, and beautiful enough. And I wasn't one of them.

Since God made a mistake, I had no choice but to fix it. For years, I embarked on a series of on-again, off-again diets, endless hours of cardio and workout classes, calorie restriction, and general berating of my body when it refused to conform to the standard I was trying to achieve. Even when I finally did make the cheerleading squad in high school, I was the girl in the bigger uniform, the size large in a group of extra smalls.

When my body refused to conform, I hid: behind layers of clothing, behind layers of makeup, behind layers of self-depricating humor, good grades, and an impressive resume of achievements to make up for what my body lacked.

My body was a battleground, and come hell or highwater, I was going to force it to surrender and shrink to a desirable size. I was exhausted, but I mustered my resolve and kept fighting.

In my mid twenties, something started to shift. Through a series of events, I found myself as a resident of a country in the South Pacific, working with children who had experienced trauma. One of the services we provided was intensive medical care for sick children. A twelve year old girl was admitted, and while I was not the one providing medical services, I was her caregiver.

Her illness left her unable to walk, and she needed help getting to the bathroom. I remember on one particular day, I crouched beside her, scooped her into my arms, and carried her to where she needed to be.

Thank God for my thighs.

The thought was random, almost intrusive, but it stopped me in my tracks. I had never thanked God for any part of my body, much less my thighs, for which I usually carried extra special disdain.

However, in this moment, I recognized that my thighs were giving me the ability to lift this little girl and meet her needs. Those thighs might have secured me a forever spot at the bottom of a cheerleading pyramid, but in this moment, they were exactly what they needed to be to help a child.

That small thought, like a tiny spark, eventually flamed into a new way of thinking. "What if," I almost dared myself to ask, "God didn't make a mistake?"

Ephesians 2:10 seems to confirm this. "For we are God's handiwork, created in Christ Jesus to do good works, which God prepared in advance for us to do."

Handiwork: work that is done by hand. "Prepared in advance" meaning, there was a plan (Ephesians 2:10)? My journey changed course, and I began to think about what it meant to surrender my body to God, to accept the intentionality of his design. A funny thing happened when I began to do this.

I found peace.

In a twist of irony, I found that when I stopped fighting against my body and started fighting with it, I found purpose, meaning, and yes, peace in the work I was designed to do. Eating became a way to fuel my body, rather than punish it. Exercise became a celebration of what I could do instead of torture. Rest felt more like a life-giving well, instead of a guilty pleasure.

My peace with my body became a gift I could share with others. I taught the children I worked with how to exercise. I learned to care for my health so I could handle the stress of an intense job.

Later, when I became a mother, my body was cared for and treasured as the source of life for my developing babies.

As part of this gift, I get to help my children develop a mindset of peace instead of war over their bodies and God's design.

We often hear that we are more than our bodies, but that does not erase the pain and shame we have felt because of our bodies. This pain and shame matters, and I am sure, like me, you have developed your own wounds and scars.

Friend, I want to invite you to join me on the journey to accept the body you have been given. I invite you to think of the ways you have used your body to do the good works God has prepared you to do. Have your hips carried children in a piggy back ride? Have your knees spent time in the dirt in desperate prayer? Have your arms wrapped a friend closely in comfort? Have your legs carried you down an aisle to be joined with your best friend in marriage or to the breathtaking view of a mountaintop sunrise?

Yes, you are more than your body, but what an unbelievable gift you are to the world when you are at peace with your body. It is time to look in the mirror and stop the fight.

Jordan Horvath, PhD, LCSW is a Licensed Clinical Social Worker and holds a doctorate in Child Development. She wears many hats, but usually while watching college football and sipping iced coffee. Of all her roles, her favorite is being a wife and mom, and a reluctant chicken owner.

THE TELLTALE HEART AND THE STILL SMALL VOICE

Briane Pittman Kearns

I lay in the MRI tube, my legs secured by Velcro, my arms above my head. The sound of the machine whirred loudly, despite the protective earplugs. Multiple ECG electrodes connected around my heart and chest. A blood pressure cuff periodically squeezed my arm, making me jump despite the restraints, while additional monitors tracked my pulse and breathing.

Two other noises filled my ears. The first was the commands of the MRI technicians. "Breathe," "Hold your breath," "Breathe again" throughout the scan.

The second was the sound of my own heartbeat, broadcast loudly into the MRI and command rooms. *Whoosh-thump. Whoosh-thump. Whoosh-thump.* I felt as if I were in Poe's story "The Tell-Tale Heart."

I was strapped in this tube because five days earlier, I had been blindsided by a diagnosis: Class III Heart Failure, with a leaky valve, and a life-threatening blood clot in the bottom of my left ventricle.

As a two-time breast cancer survivor, I have sat in consultation rooms and heard bad news. But this diagnosis was a complete shock; no one in my family has ever had heart issues. I was terrified. This cardiac

MRI was the first of many tests to determine why and how much my heart was failing.

Fear overpowered me in that MRI tube, paralyzing my mind. I was unable to recall treasured Bible verses that reassured me in past difficulties. Strapped down, breathing on command, I was desperate for the soothing words of God.

And then, as clearly as I heard my own heartbeat, I heard the voice of Jesus: "Peace I leave with you. My peace I give to you" (John 14:27), cutting through all the noise was the "still, small voice" from Scripture, quiet and personal (1 Kings 19:12 KJV).

Jesus gave me His peace when I could not grasp it myself. Over and over, I repeated "Jesus, I take hold of your peace." And peace filled me as I inhaled and exhaled on cue for 90 minutes.

After the test concluded, I kept thinking about Jesus' words. In His promise made to His disciples in the Upper Room, peace is not an intangible thing; it is something that can be left, something that can be given to someone.

As a Bible teacher, I needed to understand what had just happened to me. I took a deep dive into Biblical peace. I learned that the peace Jesus gave me that day was far more profound and costly than I had previously understood. Hang with me for a minute while I get nerdy, because it's worth it.

The Bible uses two words for peace: the Hebrew *shâlôm* and the Greek *eirēne*. Though from different cultures, both communicate the same profound meaning. They describe something far richer than mere absence of conflict. They encompass complete well-being, wholeness, the deep satisfaction that comes when body, soul, and spirit are thriving.

Shâlôm especially emphasizes bodily health, while *eirēne* connects closely to salvation. Both point to the good that comes from God in this age and the next. This peace is also directly connected to a covenant relationship with God.

Throughout the Old Testament, people wished peace upon one another, not as empty greetings, but as prayers for genuine well-being and freedom from trouble. Yet they knew peace wasn't free. The peace offerings commanded by God in Leviticus required the sacrifice of an unblemished animal. Blood had to be shed to present this offering.

This was a stark reminder to them (and to us) that true peace costs life itself.

But the blood of animals merely pointed to what was needed to bring true peace. Through His death on the cross, Jesus became the perfect sacrifice, paying the ultimate price for peace once and for all time. Jesus brings peace through His life, death, and resurrection. And thus, He can give it to me, and to you as well.

Jesus spoke peace frequently into people's lives. After healing a woman with a bleeding disease, Jesus concluded their encounter saying, "Go in peace" (Luke 8:48). When a sinful woman washed His feet during a Pharisee's tension-filled dinner, Jesus said to her, "Your faith has saved you; go in peace" (Luke 7:50). These weren't mere social pleasantries. They were spiritual blessings. Jesus was bestowing *shâlôm* well-being to these women.

In Jesus' post-resurrection greetings to His disciples, He repeatedly said, "Peace be with you" (John 20:21). This was more than a "hello." Jesus was giving them the ultimate, eternal peace that He gives to those who join His victory over death.

This ultimate peace is the fulfillment of Jesus' promise to them, "Peace I leave with you; my peace I give to you" (John 14:27). In a time of uncertainty and confusion after His death and resurrection, Jesus gave them tranquility, harmony, and security, even as they continued to live in a troubled world. He gave it to me in that MRI tube.

The peace Jesus gave me that day wasn't mere comfort or the absence of danger. It was *shâlôm* itself: divine wholeness when body, soul, and spirit thrive together. It's the breathtaking paradox of gospel peace: we can be simultaneously broken and whole, dying and fully alive. This means I can live abundantly, even with a failing heart. Yes, I still face medical uncertainty and fearful days. But intentionally taking hold of Christ's peace enables me to experience profound wholeness despite my broken heart.

When 'what-ifs' crowd my mind, I return to that tube moment: "Jesus, I take hold of your peace." It's not wishful thinking or a denial of my physical reality. It's connection to a deeper reality. He promises not necessarily more years, but complete well-being in whatever time I have, and beyond. This is the *shâlôm* Jesus died to restore, the wholeness that awaits every broken heart that takes hold of His gift.

Praise be to the One who spoke peace into that sterile tube, who has gifted peace to me at the cost of His own life.

Briane Pittman Kearns takes the boring out of Bible study and brings God's Word to life. A Gordon-Conwell Seminary graduate, she writes and teaches studies that help readers experience Scripture in its historical and cultural context. A Southerner, she loves laughing with friends and avoids cooking whenever possible.

WHEN PEACE
WRAPS THE HEART

Angel Harrell King

The cold shadows danced outside the window. I sat frozen in the hospital room, watching the trees trade light for darkness. My mind was numb, and my heart felt paralyzed. How could our 21-month-old baby, the gifted miracle after two pregnancy losses, be starving? The pediatrician's words echoed in the sterile room, "Justin's weight is now what he weighed at nine months, and we still do not have a diagnosis."

We tried everything. New formulas. Specialists. Nothing helped. Our sweet boy's hair grew thin and coarse, his face swollen, his eyes sunken. Justin looked like a child from a distant famine, and no one could tell us why.

If you have ever prayed with desperate hope and received an answer you didn't want, you know the spiritual chaos I lived in: hope and fear, brave faith one day and fierce anger the next. I prayed that God would heal Justin. I pleaded. I begged.

When heaven seemed silent, I discovered something the hard way: peace is not the absence of suffering. It is finding security in the faithful presence of God within it. God was always there, whether or not my heart could sense Him. But surrendering to His sovereign plan terrified me. The answer to my prayers was not always the solution I wanted; often it was a needed refocus and His call to surrender.

Slowly, surrender began to open my clenched hands and heart to a greater reality. I learned to say, "I want what You want, God, even if it isn't the 'yes' to my prayers." Those words were excruciating, yet they began to release something inside me I knew I needed: a greater level of trust, a bold faith, a confidence in what I could not see. I stopped measuring God by the size of my relief. My simple, raw prayer eventually became "I know You can heal Justin. I pray You will. Help me to love and trust You the same if You don't."

This kind of letting go was not one dramatic act but a daily habit to develop. Some mornings my panic returned before breakfast. On those days, I practiced one small thing: I shifted my focus. Instead of looping through "why" and "what if," I anchored one truth: God loves my child more than I do, and His ways reach beyond my understanding. I loosened my grip and leaned in with new trust. This became a rhythm of refocus and release.

This regular rhythm helped me understand that peace is not situational; it's continual, available at *all* times for *every* circumstance. Paul wrote in 2 Thessalonians 3:16a, "Now may the Lord of peace himself give you peace at all times and in every way."

These truths became my counter-rhythm to fear, reshaping how I understood peace itself. When I opened my hands, I noticed something unexpected: peace was closer than I had ever imagined. This did not mean life became easy. His peace gave me the strength I needed when life remained hard.

In Philippians 4:7, Paul reminds us the peace of God "will guard your hearts and minds in Christ Jesus." The Greek word for "guard" means more than to defend; it means to surround. Imagine being wrapped, not just behind a shield of protection, but in a living presence—warm, encircling. This peace doesn't ignore the trial; it holds the heart steady through it.

His presence didn't keep pain away. It let me cry and rage with God while He comforted me in my sorrow and disappointment. This honest lament became a sacred space where faith was strengthened. It allowed me to hold grief and gratitude together: gratitude for a child given after loss and grief for the limits of his frail body. When my hands and heart were open, I could receive His peace, not because circumstances changed, but because my heart was drawn to His and my trust was growing.

This perspective helped me see things differently. His grace arrived in small mercies: a compassionate physician, a timely message from a friend, a surprising moment of laughter. These were not answers, they were reminders: evidence that God was present, even when resolution remained distant.

God does not always answer prayers the way we hope or think He should. Justin did not become an emblem of health overnight. There were many specialists, countless tears, multiple surgeries, and endless nights of anguished pleading.

Yet as the years passed, the desired outcomes I had made essential to my peace transitioned to an unwavering confidence in God Himself. I recognized His peace is not fragile. It is fierce, more fierce than my anger once was. With it, I could hold both sorrow and trust, both ache and awe. The peace He gave through these trials didn't erase Justin's vulnerabilities; it changed my posture toward them.

God's invitation is not to a life without pain but to His perfect peace that can wrap our hearts through pain. Open your hands. God can hold what we were never meant to carry alone.

My prayer is now shaped more by surrender than certainty: *Lord, I bring You my restless heart. Teach me to trust when clarity is withheld and time feels cruel. Wrap my heart and mind with Your peace, the peace beyond my understanding. Help me release what I cannot control and cling to You instead. You already know the outcome that will be for Your glory.*

This prayer still rises often. Each time it does, I am reminded that peace is not found in having everything explained, but having our hearts and minds faithfully guarded in Christ as we bring each situation to Him.

Angel Harrell King is an author, speaker, and Master Life Coach. With rich ministry experience, she brings compassionate clarity to her writing, speaking, and coaching. A trusted voice, Angel helps her clients renew perspective and rediscover hope with practical guidance that inspires transformation. Connect at angelkingcoaching.com, Instagram, and Facebook.

TAKING CARE

Christine King

Looking back, it was all so obvious. The excuses. The cancelled plans. The busy schedules. It was no one's fault. But somehow, without even noticing, we'd been apart for almost a year. And now I was driving through a blizzard on an icy, abandoned interstate, desperate to reach my mother who was lying injured and alone in a hospital bed.

I followed the snow-packed tire tracks ahead of me, gripping the steering wheel with white knuckles, frantically praying. "Lord, forgive me. How was I so blind? Please help me. Please keep me on this road. I need to stay on this road." Fear slithered and coiled in my gut, banding across my chest, winding snakelike into a stranglehold around my neck. "What am I going to do? Oh Lord, what am I going to do?"

As snow pelted the windshield and wind grabbed the tires, God answered my crazed plea with an imperceptible "Breathe." The first ragged inhale relaxed my shoulders and a shaky, uneven exhale loosened the frenzy-induced vice on my heart. The second breath went stronger and deeper as my mind shook loose a scripture, long memorized and forgotten, to take the place of my fear filled mantra.

"... whatever is true, whatever is noble, whatever is right, whatever is pure, whatever is lovely, whatever is admirable—if anything is excellent or praiseworthy—think about such things. Whatever you have learned or received or heard from me, or seen in me—put it into practice. And the God of peace will be with you."

(Philippians 4:8-9)

Over and over again, the powerful words looped through my mind, my dread softly diminishing as the pure, noble, and lovely thoughts planted by God replaced my panic with peace.

I confess memorizing Bible verses has been more an act of obedience than devotion. My grandmother used to say, "we memorize scripture so divine truth will rise to the surface when we need it." On this ice-covered, four-hour drive, her wisdom and wise counsel steadied me in a new way. I still didn't know what I was walking into, but I was reminded that God's words of hope and evidence of protection and provision would be walking in with me.

There's a strange moment when you realize your parents are elderly. If you're lucky, the realization dawns slowly. You notice they circle the parking lot for the closest spot, you watch them hold stair railings more tightly, or you feel oddly nervous when they pull out a ladder. The harder way is more like a frying pan to the head. It's sudden and serious. Things like a winter cold changing to pneumonia in a day or a minor car accident that takes their keys. In my case, mom fell and really couldn't get up. But the precautionary trip to the doctor to check her bruised shoulder revealed a hidden illness, a growing tumor, and a terminal diagnosis. Before the fall she was just "mom." But within a few hours she'd become a frail, fragile, vulnerable old woman. And she was dying.

For the next week, we rode the current between resolution and shell shock. We called my brothers for a family meeting. Conversations led to more conversations with more questions than answers. Helping mom settle back into her home meant uncomfortable discussions about next steps, living alone, and sketching out a care plan. We got a crash course in home health care, palliative care, and hospice. We cried together and on our own, but even impending death didn't mean we'd pull any punches during games of gin rummy or stop battling to shout out the winning answers on TV quiz shows.

Caring for someone who is dying required years of experience I didn't have. Paying attention and being on alert 24/7 is exhausting. In the onslaught of medical and emotional issues, obvious-to-me solutions were often painful or difficult for reasons I hadn't considered. Medicine takes away pain, but reduces clarity. The wheelchair makes outings more efficient, but steals independence. I learned pain can look like anger. Or pity. Or bitterness. Or accusation. Or pain.

Other parts were less complicated: cooking, cleaning, wound care, staying on top of the schedule, notes, and communication. As in real life, the daily responsibilities could easily fill every minute. What was oddly difficult was remembering to stop and be still. Remembering that spending time with mom is the important stuff.

Before all this happened, I never understood my mom in her sitting. How she could sit in her living room, look out the window, and watch the birds, happy to have nothing else to do. At home, my backyard is a nagging chore of too-tall grass and shaggy bushes I keep intending to turn into an English garden. But when I sat quietly with my mom, in her cozy, velvet grandma chairs, the backyard became a wonderland. We would watch with delight, giggling at the rabbits' silly games and reprimanding the squirrels' thievery as the birds swooped and chattered above their heads. It was quiet. It was peaceful. It was stunningly beautiful.

My mom is gone now. But caring for her left me with gifts that have changed me for the better. It was the place where I learned to be patient in a new way. Slowing down let my "gentleness be evident to all" and experiences like driving through the blizzard reminded me terror cannot exist where prayer and truth reside (Philippians 4:5). I learned peace is not a place or even a destination. It's a moment. It's a gift. It's noticing the beauty hiding in plain sight outside your window. It's the ability to find the joy in the struggle and choosing to set your mind on what is true, right, and noble. In the end, it's the miraculous side effect of giving your heart, mind, and soul to God.

Christine King is a wife, mother, and wordsmith transitioning from her longtime role of "onefunmom3" to "What's Next!" Grounded in faith and passionate about kindness, her happy place is waiting to board an airplane for her next big adventure. lifeinthesandwich@gmail.com

BUILD HER UP
IN TRUTH AND LOVE:
RESTORING PEACE AMONG
SISTERS IN CHRIST

Danielle Lampman

"Grace, mercy and peace from God the Father and from Jesus Christ, the Father's Son, will be with us in truth and love."

—2 John 1:3

It's a strange thing, walking into a room when you know you've been talked about. You feel it. Conversations turn to whispers. Smiles tighten. You can sense who's heard it, who repeated it, and who believed it but didn't have the courage to ask if it was true.

It's not always the words themselves that hurt most. It's the silence of those who knew better and said nothing. Words that should have been silenced were masked as concern, dismantling relationships that once felt safe. "Do not let any unwholesome talk come out of your mouths, but only what is helpful for building others up according to their needs, that it may benefit those who listen" (Ephesians 4:29-32).

Now, when you walk into the room, you're the leper, the unclean one, a cautionary tale whispered about in the name of fellowship. You feel it in every hesitant glance, every half-hug that ends too soon, and every conversation that pauses when you walk by. No one wants to be the one seen standing with you, laughing with you, or sitting beside you.

You long for peace, but it seems impossible. You retreat, burying your God-given gifts alongside the hurt and rejection. Your voice made to help, nurture, encourage, and build up the body of Christ is now too fearful to speak, too crushed to disciple, and too guarded to allow anyone close. The peace you once rested in has now turned into a constant vigilance that exhausts your soul.

Sister, your story doesn't end in loss. Jesus lives to intercede for His bride. The same God who heard the whispers in the temple courts still hears them today. The same Jesus who touched the leper still moves toward the woman everyone else rejects.

The teardown brings the ache of what you've lost, the friends who no longer call, the seat at the table that used to be yours, the silence where laughter once lived. That emptiness makes you wonder if your peace will ever be restored.

That's where Jesus meets you, in the brokenness. He brushes back the ashes that used to be your confidence, the splinters of misplaced trust, and He begins walking through the ruins with you. He doesn't tell you to get over it. He tells you to look at it, to see it for what it is, because truth can't rebuild what you refuse to admit is broken. "Your people will rebuild the ancient ruins and will raise up the age-old foundations; you will be called Repairer of Broken Walls, Restorer of Streets with Dwellings" (Isaiah 58:12).

The rebuilding begins when you stop replaying all the things they said about you. You renew your mind and stand firm in truth. It may be slow at first, a verse that lands differently than it used to, a prayer you didn't think you had the strength to pray. One day, you awake to that wound healed, and a scar left to bear witness to the one who promised never to leave you or forsake you.

Where they once said "Too much," He whispers, "Chosen."

Where they said, "Hard to love," He says, "Mine."

Where they said, "Don't trust her," He says, "I have plans for her."

You forgive them. Not because it didn't hurt, but because you refuse to let what others said about you echo louder than Christ's righteousness over you. You make peace with them because the Holy Spirit in you refuses to let the enemy divide the family of God for one moment longer.

Sometimes the greatest witness you will ever be is the one who loves and prays for those who persecute you, believing God can still change them.

This is my testimony.

I am you.

Sadly, at times I've been one of them too.

We need to be women who build one another up in truth and love, and protect the peace within our communities.

Then, Lord willing, we will find ourselves seated at the same table, not as rivals but as sisters, breaking bread and realizing the impossible has been made possible. We no longer see the one who wounded us, but the one on whom God's grace was poured out on.

To the woman who still shows up even when it's hard, who continues to stand up in spaces that once wounded you, I see you. Keep showing up because the Holy Spirit in you carries something precious that others desperately need. One day, someone will walk into that room holding the same pain you once carried, and you will see her and hug her long enough for her to know it's safe.

You become living proof that truth and love can restore peace between sisters, and the very words meant to tear you down can become a testimony that sets others free.

Danielle Lampman is an author and speaker. Bold in faith and rooted in truth and love, she carries a message that heals, affirms women's identity in Christ, and encourages intimacy with Jesus. She builds up with the Word and equips women to do Kingdom work. For more, visit daniellelampman. com.

TEA, TEARS, AND THE TENDERNESS OF GOD

Liz Lassa

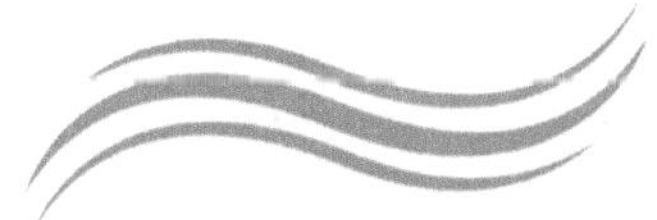

It was December of 2021. I sat hunched over my journal, sharing my heart with God. I was startled when a vision flashed into my mind of a scared little girl jumping away as a bomb exploded. She shielded her tear-stained eyes with her arm as she looked back at the destruction and loss.

I sat up straight as if struck by lightning as a realization hit me. I was that child, and I was living in a constant state of tension, always bracing for the next bomb to drop. Not literally, but emotionally. My lack of peace was unsettling.

Many people I loved dearly were dealing with serious health issues. The scariest was my mother's two-year battle with stage-four lung cancer. It didn't help that we had all just experienced the craziness of 2020. I lacked the peace I craved.

Boom! I sank into my chair as I heard the next bomb go off. A PET scan revealed that my mom's lung cancer had progressed.

My mom has always been more than a parent: she's my person, my safe place, the one I call when I need advice. She is a godly woman with the spiritual gift of wisdom, and she's never steered me wrong. Mom has always been there for me. A few days after her health update, I came upon a random, but encouraging devotional titled, "Keep Calm & Carry On."

I was curious about the story behind the popular phrase. A little Googling revealed it was from a poster created by the British administration during World War II to boost morale and help keep people calm as bombs dropped on their cities. Two million posters were printed by the British government, but this slogan was never used and pulped due to a paper shortage. A few posters survived, and 61 years later, one was found in a Northumberland bookstore. Before long, the saying began appearing on merchandise.

The timing of this slogan appearing in my life resonated and brought me peace. When I first learned of my mom's cancer in 2019, I lived in a numb, lifeless "cancer fog" for months that made it hard to accomplish anything. I let the sadness consume me. This new bomb dropped right before Christmas of 2021 when I was in the middle of a few ministry projects. I needed to finish them before I got on a plane to visit my family in Florida for what might be my last Christmas with both of my parents.

I could not allow this recent cancer report to take me out again. To help keep myself calm, I painted a little orange canvas with the popular slogan on it and placed it over my kitchen sink. My former retreat partner had taught me the value of creating art to keep an important message front and center. I didn't share it with anyone. The message was only for me.

Soon after that, my mom's group mentor dropped off two Christmas presents. She gave me her gift and I opened it in front of her. I closed the door and opened the second bag. It was from a leader of the group. Inside was a red coffee mug that said, "Keep Calm and Carry On."

Wow! Could that be a coincidence? I did a little digging and discovered the mug was an unused door prize leftover from the meeting, and on a whim, they said to the mentor, "Please give this to Liz since she missed the Christmas meeting." A devotional, a canvas I was inspired to paint, and a mug with the same message placed into my hands! I think God was encouraging me to "Keep Calm and Carry On." I chose to take a few deep breaths, relax, and let the cup's message settle into my soul as I completed my projects.

Several years have passed since that frightening Christmas season and my mom's bad prognosis. After a couple years of treatment, her cancer has not spread and is barely showing up on her scans. Who knew that was even possible with stage-four cancer? My mom still continues her checkups, but she is stable and enjoying a good life. Praise God! The cancer hasn't won!

Now, when I wrap my hands around my red mug and take that first slow sip, warmth and gratitude spread through my heart. This mug reminds me of God's tenderness as He showed up with the perfect message to bring me peace when I desperately needed it.

Isaiah 41:10 says, "So do not fear, for I am with you; do not be dismayed, for I am your God. I will strengthen you and help you; I will uphold you with my righteous right hand."

When life blindsides us, and it will because that's the nature of living in a broken world, we are never left to face life on our own. We are invited to choose. Will we be anxious or will we let the Holy Spirit soothe our souls like a warm cup of tea? I hope that you'll grab your favorite mug, brew up a steaming mug of chamomile, take a few deep breaths, and with God's help, "Keep Calm and Carry On."

Liz Lassa is a speaker, retreat leader, and life purpose coach. A widow and mother of three, she inspires women to connect deeply with God through Spiritual Circle Journaling. Liz lives in the Chicagoland area and loves hosting fun gatherings, traveling, painting, and cooking with family. Contact her at www.LizLassa.com.

EMERGENCY: PSALM 91:1

Paula LeJeune

The buzz of my husband's cell phone was almost unnoticed under the clatter of forks, the girls bantering, and the sizzle of bacon grease. The radio played uplifting Christian lyrics, and our black-and-white shih tzu tossed her one-eyed stuffed bear in the air, leaping to catch it again.

An early morning call was not uncommon. We were in our sixth year of pastoring and almost everyone in our small congregation had his cell phone number.

Clifton answered the phone. On the other end was his mother's oncologist, explaining that her lungs were failing and she needed to be put on a ventilator. Within seconds, the atmosphere in the kitchen changed.

The girls, ages 6 and 9, didn't understand the gravity of the phone call, but their hushed chatter told me they sensed the urgency.

Fearing it would be his last chance to hear Carol Ann's voice, Clifton asked the doctor to delay the procedure until he arrived. He kissed the girls on their heads, then pressed his lips to mine. Moments later, he was gone, choosing his motorcycle instead of his truck, hoping the ride would offer a brief mental escape.

After Cliff left, I steadied my nerves with routine: dropping the girls at school and coming home to clean. The radio kept me company as I dusted furniture and swept floors, its soothing songs helping me hold things together. My fragile peace was short-lived.

An emergency alert interrupted a worship song, and I dismissed it as just a test. When the alert sounded again, I turned up the volume. Then froze. The announcer was describing the devastation at the Twin Towers in New York City.

My mother-in-law was dying, the United States was under attack, and Clifton knew none of it. This was a fear I would have to deal with by myself.

My knees gave way beneath me, and I sank to the living room floor. Screaming into a sofa pillow, I poured out my fears to a God I couldn't see but needed to trust. My Bible sat on the shelves in the living room, and I reached for it. Drowning, I clung to it like a life raft.

Turning to Psalm 91:1–2, I stepped out of the panic and into His presence, making that passage personal: "Whoever dwells in the shelter of the Most High will rest in the shadow of the Almighty. I will say of [You], Lord, '[You] are my refuge and my fortress, my God, in whom I trust.'"

For the first time that week, my mind stopped racing long enough to breathe.

Then the ringing of my cell phone startled me back to reality. It was Clifton, responding to the missed phone calls from me. I filled him in on the unmitigated attack of terrorism happening in our country.

Between his mother's decline, our shaken nation, and the strain of leading a church, even simple chores felt impossible.

By week's end, the nerves that routine life protected were exposed and raw.

Saturday evening, the girls were asleep and Cliff and I were discussing plans for the following day. He remembered a commitment he had made earlier in the week that he forgot to tell me about. The addendum to our crowded Sunday agenda became my breaking point. I snapped at him then refused to talk.

Defeated by my loud silence, Cliff grabbed his pillow from the bed and announced he was heading to the church to pray and would sleep in his office. He had to get his head together before speaking to our congregation the next day.

Before his wheels exited our driveway, my thoughts were spiraling. He had never left me before. Anger welled up inside of me. Frustrated, I opened the dryer door and yanked yesterday's clothes from the drum. Slamming the door gave me a strange sense of relief. I began slapping shorts, t-shirts, and socks around before shoving them into their respective drawers.

This chaos was familiar. It was my childhood norm, where irrational thoughts and behaviors were normalized. Resentment settled in, reopening old wounds.

My heart said, "Talk to God," but the voice in my head said, "He won't hear you if you do."

As if on cue, fragmented clips began playing in my head. Scenes of me as a child, cowering on a bathroom floor, waiting for blows from my angry father's belt. I screamed for help. Nothing.

I made a half-hearted attempt at praying to the God who I had found security with only days before. "Did you lose our address? Can't you see how much pressure we are under? Cliff is at the church and I'm stuck here and can't make this right . . ."

I sounded childish, even to myself. The stream of tears blurred my vision. I was once again that lost little girl: broken, abused, and abandoned.

Desperate, I prayed, "God, Cliff is talking to you right now. Can you tell him to come home? I need to talk to him."

When the washer buzzed, I moved the clothes to the dryer. As I worked, I heard Cliff's car door shut. I looked up just in time to see him walk through the door. Our eyes met; his were wet with tears.

My voice cracked as I struggled to speak, "What are you doing here?"

"God told me to come home. You needed me."

As I melted into his arms, peace flooded my heart. Nothing around us had changed, but God had heard me. He hadn't lost our address after all. He had done exactly as He promised at the end of Psalm 91: "He will call on me, and I will answer him; I will be with him in trouble, I will deliver him and honor him. With long life, I will satisfy him and show him my salvation" (Psalm 91:15-16).

Paula LeJeune, author of *The Perfectly Imperfect Princess* and *Perfectly Imperfect* has pastored alongside her husband, Clifton, for over thirty years. Married for 37 years, she shares heartfelt stories of faith, grace, and authenticity from their life and ministry in a small town in south Louisiana.

PEACE IN THE UNKNOWN

Racquel Lopez

I stood at a crossroads: keep living the same way or step into a new life I couldn't yet imagine. Both paths terrified me. One familiar and destructive, the other uncharted and uncertain. I remember sitting in rehab realizing something had to change. I didn't know it then, but choosing the unknown would lead me to a peace I never thought possible.

To understand how I got there, you have to know where it all began.

I grew up in church, but somewhere along the way I believed the lie that Christians had to be perfect and I was already too far gone. By the time I entered high school, I wasn't a virgin, and I started drinking to numb my feelings. I lived in fear of being exposed, my stomach dropping whenever I was questioned about the night before. Shame told me I was damaged goods, so I buried the longing to change, but it never stopped tugging at me.

After high school, everything started falling apart fast. When I looked in the mirror, I didn't even recognize the girl staring back. I failed classes, quit soccer (the reason I went to college) lost a job, blacked out more times than I could count, and eventually landed in rehab after a DUI. But leaving rehab didn't magically fix me. I went back to my old patterns, and the pain only deepened. On the surface, it didn't seem like my world was collapsing. My life looked normal enough, friends, school, and college partying, right? But in the quiet moments, waking up on strangers' couches with bruises I couldn't explain, pretending to remember nights I couldn't, surrounded by people yet completely alone, I felt the emptiness. I didn't recognize it then, but looking back, I see God's mercy was already waiting.

Time passed, but the pain didn't, and everything I'd been running from finally caught up with me. Another DUI, broken relationships, and destruction were all around me. I was exhausted and trapped in choices I hated, unable to see a way out.

But one night everything changed. I came home and told my mom I didn't want to live this way anymore. I asked for help and for the first time in years, I felt a tiny flicker of hope. For years, fear kept me stuck. But that night, I realized staying the same terrified me more than the unknown ever could.

The psalmist gave language to what I couldn't express:

The ropes of death entangled me; floods of destruction swept over me. The grave wrapped its ropes around me; death laid a trap in my path. But in my distress I cried out to the Lord; yes, I prayed to my God for help. He heard me from his sanctuary; my cry to him reached his ears.

(Psalm 18:4–6 NLT)

The first night of my second stay in rehab, I whispered a shaky prayer, the first honest words I'd spoken to God in years. I didn't know what to say or how to make my life right. But as soon as I surrendered, something shifted. I felt lighter, relaxed, calm, and finally at peace. That peace wasn't my doing, it was His grace meeting me in surrender. The same God I thought I'd run too far from, met me right where I was. I was the one running from His love, His calling, and the truth. The peace He gave me that night was enough to take one step at a time, one day, one moment, toward a different life.

I began a personal relationship with Jesus, talking to Him like a friend, learning to trust His voice in the quiet, and though my life didn't change overnight, my story started moving in a completely different direction. Slowly, God pieced me back together into the woman I never thought I could be, one with peace, healthy relationships, purpose, and the deep knowledge that she was loved.

Looking back, I realize how deeply I'd misjudged God. I thought He expected perfection. I thought He was waiting to punish me. But instead, He delighted in me, even in my brokenness. He didn't delight in my sin, but in redeeming me, His daughter whom He never stopped loving. I learned firsthand that His promises are real. "God's way is perfect. All the Lord's promises prove true. He is a shield for all who look to him for protection" (Psalm 18:30 NLT).

That's what I found in surrender: a shield, a refuge, and a peace that didn't depend on my circumstances.

He rebuilt me from the inside out, piece by piece, as I learned to trust Him and take steps of faith in His direction. It began with honesty, admitting what wasn't working and surrendering what I couldn't fix. God used self-reflection to reveal patterns and lies, and community to keep me accountable and supported. My job was obedience and gratitude; His was the rest.

Each one moved me closer to peace. They weren't overnight fixes, but daily choices that strengthened my faith. It reminds me that when life starts spinning again or old wounds flare up, He's got me. He always has and always will.

You don't have to have it figured out. God already does.

So where do you need change? What feels hopeless or impossible right now? It could be addiction, anxiety, or a secret shame you've carried too long, but the thing you think God can't touch, He can heal. He will guide you one step at a time. The unknown may feel terrifying, but it's often the very place God meets us.

These days, peace doesn't mean my life is perfect, it means I know Who is with me in it. Wherever you are, no matter how far gone you feel, God can do for you what He did for me.

Take His hand and step into the unknown, because that's exactly where peace begins.

Racquel Lopez helps women, especially moms, break free from shame, fear, and old identities to experience the hope, healing, and purpose found in Jesus. Through her recovery story, speaking, and counseling, she encourages others to live resilient lives. She's wife to Anthony and mom to Trinity, Olivia, Paul, and Violet.

JUST BREATHE, GOD SEES

Mallory Lynch

My feet dragged on the gravel road. My chest tightened. Two and a half years sober, but the bottle called my name, and instead of asking for help, I put the bottle to my lips. My wrists were thin. Too thin. My eyes were dark and hollow. A voice spoke loudly in my ear, "You have no value. Why are you even trying?" I remembered how my mom covered me in prayer not to lose myself. This gravel road felt like Death Valley, and I was utterly lost. One drink leading to many threw me back toward broken trust, back to the place where I found the bottle more valuable than love. My mom was the one God used to speak life into my dry bones. I had forgotten how to breathe. I didn't know three honest words could save me.

Nothing looked familiar. I craved oxygen. My chest was tight. My legs trembled as the voice whispered, "Could you stay sober this time? How long until you hurt everyone again?" The shame overwhelmed me as the voice screamed, "Why don't you give up already? You already failed and drank."

Trapped in time, tears rolled down my face as I realized I was covered in mud. My body felt disconnected in slow motion. It was like watching someone else reach into my pocket as my fingers wrapped around the handle. I pressed it against my left wrist. But then the sharp pain came. I looked down. Red. My wrist throbbed; I dropped the knife, frozen in time. What had I done?

Then I remembered how I protected my dad, but I did not understand alcoholism and his demons. Was I hearing the same voices he fought? My body shook as the voices grew louder. My parents' faces were all I could see. Then I looked down at my wrist; all of this was too much. I wondered, "How do I get out of this?" I prayed as fear tried to paralyze me. As the wind blew, my hair hit my face sharply, reminding me I was not alone. Somehow, I was seen. In the chaos, a small gentle voice—not audible, but unmistakable—whispered: "I can rescue you, lean into me." My chest expanded as air filled my lungs. I heard, "Just breathe."

I'd spent years attending meetings, yet I never changed. People would know I was a fake. I wondered, *Can I be honest? I only know how to lie.* I pulled out the heaviest phone I'd ever held. I stared down and knew who I had to call: my dad. Would I be strong enough to hear his voice when he heard mine?

I remembered defending him when I was a kid. "He's just tired," I'd tell my mom and sisters. I didn't understand that he was gone in the bottle. I resented the bottle and the man from my childhood. And now, I did not think I would ever call him for help.

Slowly, I lifted the phone to my ear. It started to ring once, then twice. Then a casual "hello." The tone shifted when he heard my shaking breath. Then silence.

I wept. There was stillness as my brittle bones trembled when three little words, "I need help," left my lips.

"Where are you?" he asked, fighting to keep his voice steady. "I'm on a gravel road near the woods. Dad, I—I can't do this anymore. I want to give up." I had forgotten God sees gravel roads and broken girls.

Silence. Then my dad's voice cracked, "We can hide you in the woods. I'll find you." He knew my struggle because his dad fought the same demons, and he wanted to protect me, hiding me from the questions. But hiding wasn't going to save me this time. Tears poured out. I couldn't remember the last time I could breathe without a struggle. Something tightened around my chest constantly. But now a miracle washed over me; the pressure was releasing. As air filled my lungs, my mouth opened. Then I remembered the verse: "This is what the Sovereign Lord says to these bones: I will make breath enter you, and you will come to life." (Ezekiel 37:5) This was happening: a sudden rush of air entered my lungs. Deep. Real. My ribs expanded. I exhaled, finally.

My shaking slowed. I heard the siren growing louder. The ambulance pulled up, lights flashing. My body felt lighter as my dad's truck approached, and I breathed in peace. The one person I never wanted to become came to my rescue. The one whose footprints I'd follow into bottles and broken promises saved me. Our eyes met as we both felt seen. His face was red, but his composure gave me strength. My dad was present and sober. For me. I could breathe.

Everything changed with three simple words, "I need help." This confession opened a door to peace I thought was closed forever. Today, when I forget how to breathe because of panic, I look at my wrist. The scar is covered by a tattoo of a heartbeat and the words, "Just breathe." That gravel road taught me: God sees broken girls, and He saw me, and He always does.

Today, my dad and I are sober. We're miracles because of my mother's prayers. Each day, we learn to love each other without the bottle between us. We are following in my grandfather's legacy of God's grace in redeeming the lost. I still forget how to breathe some days. But I remember that day—the ambulance lights, the peace I felt, and the way my dad showed up. And I breathe because God always sees.

Mallory Lynch loves Jesus and recovery. She was given the gift of desperation, surrendered everything, and now shows up boldly to reach out a hand to the lost and misunderstood. As a speaker, author, and poet her life is living proof there is no darkness a light can't reach.
www.misfitmasterpieces.com

GOD IS ALWAYS WORKING

Ashley Martin

Riding in the back of an ambulance through downtown Seattle was not the vacation I had imagined. The sirens cut through the city's hum as my son, Grant, lay on a gurney, pale and still, the monitors beating a rhythm that echoed my fear. I didn't yet grasp how serious his illness was, but I felt God's presence steadying me amid the chaos, reminding me I wasn't alone. The paramedic spoke calmly, his words landing like a hand on my shoulder, and a young doctor across from me offered a sympathetic smile as we bumped through Friday traffic toward Seattle Children's Hospital.

When we arrived, the medical team moved quickly. They placed Grant in room 32 of the sprawling emergency department, and I felt dwarfed by its scale and intensity. Doctors and nurses swarmed, firing clipped questions that underscored how serious his condition had become. His fever raged, his rash spread, and his heart raced in a way that tightened something deep inside me. The EpiPen he received earlier had done nothing. After hours of tests, the doctors admitted him. It was hard to believe that just twenty-four hours earlier,

Grant and I had taken selfies on the plane, excited for our family vacation.

Every summer, our family carves out two weeks to explore, mixing a city stop with the quiet majesty of a national park. This year promised Seattle's skyline and Mount Rainier's rugged beauty. I had planned every detail: the games, the hikes, the memories. But even the best-laid plans are fragile. Storms delayed my stepdaughter's flight, and my husband West stayed behind with her. Grant and I flew on alone. Faint bumps dotted his cheeks when we landed, and by morning they had worsened. He skipped breakfast, which was rare for him. At the Mariners game, beneath blue skies and perfect seats, my worry grew sharper. When we glanced over and saw him pale and slouched in his seat, we left immediately.

Back at the hotel, heat radiated from his skin. His fever was high. "Find a hospital," I told West. The nearest urgent care was only a block away. Within minutes, a nurse confirmed my fears: dangerously high fever, racing heart, spreading rash. They tried an EpiPen, but when protocol required an ambulance, the weight of it all finally sank in. Our family trip shifted from sightseeing to survival in a matter of minutes.

For the next five days, Grant lay in a hospital room, his body fighting battles I couldn't see. Each evening his fever surged, and food barely stayed down. Machines beeped beside his bed, monitoring his racing heart and shallow breaths. Yet even in the chaos, God was there. Had his symptoms worsened a day later, we would have been deep in the wilderness of a national park, hours from help. Instead, we were at one of the nation's best children's hospitals with doctors who refused to give up until they found answers. I whispered prayers of thanks for that mercy again and again.

Still, my heart ached. We were supposed to be hiking mountains and admiring emerald forests, not trapped in a sterile room while specialists puzzled over test results. By the morning of day four, hope stirred in me. At dawn, I slipped quietly out for coffee and a moment with God. I found the hospital's meditation room, still and dimly lit. In front of a simple altar and cross, I knelt, pouring out gratitude for the timing that saved Grant's life and for the first glimmers of healing. Before leaving, I wrote a few words in the prayer book for the next weary soul who might need the reminder I had just received: *God is always working! Never forget that!*

But that afternoon, Grant's progress slipped backward. His fever flared again, and the fragile hope I had been holding began to unravel. Discouragement welled up, and tears blurred my vision. Wandering the halls, I noticed a little girl in a wheelchair, her bald head and nasal tube revealing a brutal fight. Her father walked beside her, exhausted yet determined to give her a moment of light in those sterile corridors. My tears slowed. *It could be worse*, I thought. I needed to pray.

I returned to the meditation room, aching for strength. Drawn to the altar, I opened the prayer book. A single sentence stared back at me: *God is always working! Never forget that!* The sight undid me completely. I sank into the silence and wept, not in despair, but in recognition. What I had written for someone else, God had saved for me. In that moment, a deep, surrendering peace washed over me. Grant's healing would come in God's timing, not mine. I let go of the frantic need to control the outcome and rested in that truth.

That evening, something shifted. Grant's fever did not return. By morning, he kept food down, and the spark in his eyes shone again. He folded paper airplanes, laughed with his sister, and stacked Legos as if the past days had been only a bad dream. When the head doctor walked in, she smiled and said Grant would likely go home the next day. The toxins were leaving his body, and my son was finally on the road to recovery.

But the greater gift had already been given: in uncertainty, God had met me with peace that steadied my soul. Peace doesn't come from the absence of struggle but from the presence of God in the midst of it. That same peace is available to you. In your own waiting room, in the center of your storm, you don't have to wait until everything is fixed to feel His nearness. He is already there. Perhaps, like me, you'll find that peace comes not when circumstances change, but when you surrender them.

After all, the words I wrote for a stranger in that Seattle hospital prayer book became my own lifeline: *God is always working! Never forget that!*

 Ashley Martin is an author, speaker, wife, mother, and history teacher who believes words can heal, inspire, and point others toward purpose. She writes to help others live boldly and follow God's call. Based in Alabama, she enjoys traveling with her family, exploring coffee shops, and cheering "Roll Tide!" Connect with Ashley at www.ashleymartinministry.com.

KEPT IN PERFECT PEACE

Bella Miller

I was two and a half months postpartum with my firstborn when the thoughts of postpartum depression came spiraling into my mind. We were traveling back from a Christmas weekend with family in close quarters, too many stuffy noses, and an expiring maternity leave. I sat in the back seat, looking out at the western Carolina mountains as the thoughts of inadequacy, fear, and worthlessness crept in.

It would be so much easier if I went to sleep and never woke up. I'm never going to be enough. They would be better off without me.

I had struggled with depression since college, but this time was different. Motherhood changed me more than I expected. The weight of responsibility, trying to do everything perfectly was suffocating. It felt like a boulder pressed against my chest. My thoughts spiraled like a tornado.

Maternity leave ended and I went back to work with a smile plastered on my face as if I was holding it all together. I was always thinking about my son, never fully present. Only to come home and cry that I didn't get enough done. Those months of contradiction lasted far too long. My husband, Alex, was the only person who knew I was collapsing inside and something needed to change.

When we were at our son's four month wellness check and the nurse handed me the postpartum depression questionnaire, it felt pointless. I had filled it out before and always wondered if honesty mattered. Would anyone actually care? I didn't know how to put words to what I was feeling, but the weight of what I carried was too much.

When I took that dumb piece of paper, tears welled in my eyes. I felt Alex stare at me. "Be honest," was all he said. I knew what the last question would be, but that didn't make it easier. It read, "10. The thought of harming myself has occurred to me." As I held my breath, hands shaking, I checked off "yes, quite often." The weight of the last four soul crushing months came out in an exhale of peace. This was no longer a battle I was fighting on my own. Alex looked at me knowing how hard that simple act was. As my son's doctor finished the appointment, she noticed how I flagged for postpartum depression. Her response was compassionate, like she'd explained the seriousness of it many times before. Maybe I wasn't the only mom to experience these feelings.

As we walked out of that appointment, I knew the battle wasn't over, but I felt lighter knowing those loud, shameful thoughts were no longer hidden. The doctor didn't think any less of me, my husband walked proudly with our healthy son and I was no longer going to let the enemy have a hold over me. Bringing darkness into light was the first step.

A few days later I met with my doctor to ask for help. Through tears, I explained all I had been experiencing. I'll never forget her explaining what she felt as a postpartum mom. Even as an OBGYN, she knew what it was like to barely keep her head above the water. We came up with an action plan to regulate my hormones and to talk to a therapist until I could finally swim above the waves.

The next steps were unbearably hard: telling my closest people and adjusting my work schedule. Each conversation began in sobs as I tried to explain the feelings of failure as both the woman I was and the mother I'd become. The conversations always ended the same. Friends and sisters crying with me, covering me with prayer. A boss who extended grace, understanding, and a new schedule.

Change didn't happen overnight. Winter turned into spring, spring into summer and I was finally resurfacing from the black waters of depression. During those months, I began to use scripture to overcome the tiny dark voice that crept into my mind.

I learned about renewing my mind, but I had never practiced taking every thought captive to obey Christ so seriously (2 Corinthians 10:5). I wanted to break free of anxiety and depression and offer my body as a living sacrifice to the Lord in a way that was good, acceptable and perfect (Romans 12:1). When dark thoughts crept in, I took hold of them and thought "whatever is true, whatever is noble, whatever is right, whatever is pure, whatever is lovely, whatever is admirable" (Philippians 4:8). Where the enemy said I was unworthy and not enough, Jesus told me I was loved as His daughter.

Postpartum depression is something I pray I never experience again, but it has refined me. For that, I am thankful: His glory displayed through me. I also wish I could say depression is no longer my story. Even now, with a 3-year-old and 1-year-old, there are days I fight the mental battle when that little voice creeps in, telling me to give up.

Most often, the battle happens in the most ordinary place, my kitchen sink. Right above it is a window that looks into the backyard. I stand there more times than I can count, washing dishes with my thoughts everywhere. But that sink has become one of my favorite places. Over time, the windowsill filled with scripture on notecards pinned and taped. It's where I take every thought captive and fill them with hope and peace. I have cried tears of exhaustion, gritted my teeth through frustration, smiled at His faithfulness, and reread His words that remain forever true. That kitchen sink has become my place where I fight. My eyes always linger on Isaiah 26:3, "You will keep in perfect peace those whose minds are steadfast, because they trust in you." It's my mantra when my mind spirals. I recite it until my thoughts are captured, truth returns, and my perspective shifts to trusting Him to bring me to perfect peace.

Bella Miller is an author and aspiring speaker passionate about guiding women toward their identity in Jesus. With six years in ministry, she uses the gifts God has given her to draw others to Him. Bella is wife to Alex and mom to her two sweet babies, Cal and Collins.

GOD'S PEACE IN PRUNING:

LESSONS LEARNED THROUGH LOT'S WIFE

Sarah A. Mohr

Years ago, my family began attending a homeschool co-op. The people were welcoming and encouraging. The co-op challenged my kids, and it seemed like a great fit for all of us. I honestly thought my kids would graduate high school while attending. However, our season there ended abruptly and really rattled me. Life can be so unpredictable!

As my thoughts dwelled on what happened, God brought to mind the story of Lot's wife. I wondered, *Why did she look back when God told them to leave?* His instructions were clear, "Do not look back" (Genesis 19:17 ESV). Was it curiosity or a desire to return to the life she knew? It seems like an obvious choice to obey God when he warns of a certain disaster.

But perhaps we have the same tendency to look back and question why God would uproot us from what we know and all that makes us feel safe. Truth be told, I have been reluctant to move forward in other circumstances, but this was the first time God was clear on the lesson he was teaching me through it all.

When I got the letter denying our application to return, my thoughts began to swirl. Before I could fully land on how I felt, God's peace surrounded me, *I have something else planned for you.* Then my feelings emerged, sad and angry questioning brought on by the sting of rejection. I made the conscious decision to let peace continue to cover me.

Much like Lot's wife, leaving wasn't on my "to do" list. We had friends there, plus what would school look like going forward? I wonder if she thought the same thing: *What about our friends? What does the future look like without this in my life?* After all, they had lived in Sodom for nearly 20 years by this time. They had built a life there.

> And as they [the angels] brought them out, one said, "Escape for your life. Do not look back or stop anywhere in the valley. Escape to the hills, lest you be swept away" . . . "Escape there [Zoar] quickly, for I can do nothing till you arrive there" . . . But Lot's wife, behind him, looked back, and she became a pillar of salt.
>
> (Genesis 19:17, 22, 26 ESV).

Growing up, this part of the story seemed pretty straightforward. She turned her head and instantly became salt. But there is something more nuanced happening. Note the references of time mentioned throughout the story. They began their journey in the morning, and the angel had to wait for Lot to arrive in Zoar before anything could happen. So, when we read in verse 26, "Lot's wife . . . looked back", the destruction had not yet begun (Genesis 19:26 ESV).

It's entirely possible she turned around and headed back to Sodom. Truthfully, we can only speculate on what made her turn; all we know is that she did. And in doing so, she suffered the same fate as those in the city and became frozen in time as a salt statue.

How often do we look back when God has clearly moved us from a place or situation? Is it because we mourn the loss of what was and what could be? Are we afraid of the unknown? Don't allow these thoughts, feelings, and questions to cause a rift in relationship with God, but let your lament open the doors to clear communication with Him.

What has God moved you from that fights for your attention? Follow the directions given by the angels and don't look back, because that's not where peace and belonging reside. Lot's wife never got the chance to see what God had planned for them, and her demise brought about dire consequences to her family.

I have found it easier to move on when it's my choice, but if the decision is made for me, it's harder to accept. Do you feel that way too? Accepting what God has prepared for us will probably challenge our sense of place in the world. It's in the challenge that our character is shaped and molded into the image of Christ. God refines us to bring our shortcomings to the surface while the Holy Spirit counsels and guides us into a deeper relationship with our Creator.

Many times in the months following our co-op departure, I wondered, *What could I have done?* But there was nothing. It was time to move on. Through multiple Bible teachers, God confirmed my need to move to an environment where He could foster growth in me and my kids. Focusing on what I wish I still had would distract me from what He was bringing me to.

Jesus urges us to "remember Lot's wife" (Luke 17:32 ESV). Instead of returning to the place God rescued you from, look on the past with fondness for the lessons it taught you. Let's be people who desire to follow God's path of abundant life above all else.

Sarah A. Mohr is a lifelong learner—holding a BA in Intercultural Studies and a MA in Youth and Family Ministry. She is a certified Mental Health Coach and an ordained minister with the Assemblies of God. Her mission is to foster conversations that lead to restored relationships with each other and God.

WHEN PLANS FALL APART, GOD HOLDS YOU TOGETHER

Gwen Mrva

Some dates fade into the background of our memories, but Sunday, November 6, 2016, is one I'll never forget. The months leading up to this date were filled with excitement and growth. Life felt full in every direction; at home, and at work, everything was growing and moving forward. Personally, my husband and I were expecting our first little one. There were years in our marriage that we were not sure having a child would be in our future. We were excited to become parents and three of our closer couple friends were expecting little ones in the coming months.

Professionally, I was asked to step into a new role. After a summer of 30% growth in our kids ministry, it was time to update and scale our systems. Our team spent weeks updating classrooms, volunteer procedures, in-class programming, student documentation, and check-in/check-out procedures, while simultaneously planning our largest in-service event outside of Christmas services. As an event manager and Enneagram 8, I thrived in the energy of organized chaos. I loved bringing structure to moving parts, rallying people around a shared mission and building systems that allow for flexibility when the original plan falls apart.

I didn't know then that everything I'd built my life around—order, planning, and control—would soon unravel. The flexibility I taught my team would become a lesson my heart had to learn. That Saturday was filled with time with friends, shopping for a birthday gift, and a quick stop at work to check on a few last-minute details. It was one of those simple, uneventful days you don't realize will change everything. I felt some slight abdominal pain while I was out shopping. I felt more of the same pain that night and my husband encouraged me to call my doctor's office. The nurse recommended that I go directly to the hospital.

My heart sank: there was something wrong with our baby. We prayed every minute of the drive: for peace, for God's hand, for our sweet little girl to be ok. Once we arrived at labor and delivery, I was quickly checked in and the on-call doctor notified. After a series of tests and medications, we were told all we could do was wait and see. A couple hours later, the doctor explained what I felt earlier was contractions and my cervix was prematurely opening.

The medical team did everything they could to stop the contractions but there was nothing more they could do to keep labor from progressing. It still brings tears to type those words. The physical pain of labor was nothing compared to the ache of knowing we would leave the hospital with empty arms. At just over twenty weeks our little girl was born and went to meet Jesus. My heart broke at that moment. My body shook with sobs I couldn't contain. Words failed, and only moans of despair filled the room.

We had a bedroom full of baby clothes that she would not wear, toys that she would not play with, and linens that would never be placed in her crib. I did everything I thought was right: exercised regularly, ate well, worshiped Jesus and still, I could not carry a pregnancy to full term. I questioned, "How could this happen? How could all my plans just fall apart?"

In those first moments, all I could do was weep. Thankfully those cries to God and questions are not the end of my story. The beauty in my plans falling apart was discovering complete reliance on God's promises and the community of people He placed in my life. In surrender, I found peace. The kind that comes only when we realize that we're not in control. Each step of the way God showed up through His people. Throughout the hours of labor my sweet husband repeated the phrase, "As long as our faith is strong, and our marriage is strong, we can walk through anything." These words echoed in my heart for months, a gentle reminder that even in loss, God's strength and our love would carry us through.

Our senior pastors showed up at the hospital ready to stand in the hard dark space with us. When they couldn't enter my hospital room, they stayed and prayed for us in the parking lot. This simple act of love reminds me that even in the darkest places, God surrounds me through the love of others. Our village showed up in so many ways. Friends took care of our dog, cleaned our apartment, and removed the baby items. Our family cleared their calendars and traveled to be with us for weeks. Every act of love and kindness became a thread of God's grace and peace woven into the fabric of my pain.

When I think of November 6, 2016, I no longer feel heartache and despair. Now, I see all the ways that God provides for us in our deepest and darkest moments. You may not share my story of loss, but I am certain you know what it is like to grieve a part of your own story. Maybe, you long for a partner, or lost your job, or thought you would be further along in your life plan by now. I am not sure of the source of your heartache, but my prayer is that when your plans fall apart, you will look to God and take comfort in Him.

I will never know why I suffered such a hard loss, but I know that God's peace and His plan are always more than I could ever imagine. My hope is that in life's dark places, you'll pause long enough to see how gently God reaches for you, holding you together through the love and kindness of others.

Gwen Mrva is a life coach, podcast host, and corporate project manager who helps high-achieving women break free from burnout through simple, sustainable habits. A wife, mom, and lifelong learner, she blends science-backed wellness with practical systems to help women build a life they love.

PEACE AT THE BASE OF THE MOUNTAIN

Freda Neudorf

I was terrified riding through the Rocky Mountains for the first time in my early twenties. Growing up on the prairies hadn't prepared me for this. The mountains were so massive, dark, rugged, and ominous. They reminded me how small and insignificant I was.

This trip through the mountains was not what I had imagined a "mountaintop experience" would be like. Years later, sitting at the base of those mountains, I discovered what had really been making me feel small and "not enough" all along. It wasn't the mountains, but the voices that had been travelling with me since I was very young.

In grade one, my classmates labeled me "dumb" because I did not attend kindergarten. Being the shortest in my grade gave them another reason to tease me. I couldn't do many things that they could. Getting onto my desk chair took effort. The coat hook was too high. My short legs meant I couldn't keep up when they ran.

That feeling of "not enough" carried with me for a long time. I worked hard all through school and into college, determined to prove I wasn't dumb. Graduating from college with an 87 percent average didn't change anything, as I hoped it would. The voice still whispered "not good enough," and it kept reminding me of that for years.

When I was in my mid-thirties, I attended a women's weekend retreat in the foothills of the same Rocky Mountains that terrified me years before.

We were given a journal with writing prompts. During free time one afternoon, I took the journal and my Bible and headed to the riverbank. I sat down facing the mountains. One of the journal prompts directed me to Psalm 139:13-14. I read: "For you created my inmost being; you knit me together in my mother's womb. I praise you because I am fearfully and wonderfully made . . .." For the first time, I realized how important I am to God.

I finally believed it. I am important. Those childhood voices were wrong. God says I'm wonderfully made. The classmates who said I was too short to matter were wrong. God says I matter. For the first time in thirty years, I believed it. An unexplainable peace washed over me that can only come from God. I could breathe easier.

Sitting by the river, looking up at the mountain, I understood what a mountaintop experience was. It's not about reaching the peak. It's about God meeting me where I am and showing me who I'd always been: loved, significant, and wonderfully made.

For so long, I allowed negative thoughts to rule how I saw myself. I knew God loved me, but for the first time, I experienced it. I was fearfully and wonderfully made. I was in awe of God's love for me.

I certainly thought I was alone in believing I was unworthy and insignificant. But over time, through conversations and listening to podcasts, I've heard countless women who carry similar wounds and believe they don't measure up. It's both encouraging and heartbreaking. Encouraging because I'm not alone in this. Heartbreaking because none of us have to live this way. God's truth is available to all of us.

That afternoon by the river changed everything, yet it looked ordinary. No lightning bolts, no dramatic moments, just me, a Bible, and some quiet time with God. I'd read those same verses before, but this time they came alive. Sometimes breakthrough comes in the stillness when we're finally ready to hear God.

The voices from the past still linger. Sometimes they are just annoying background noise. Other times they demand my attention. I can choose to listen to the lies, or fill my mind with God's truth through reading the Bible, speaking memorized verses, listening to worship music, and praying Scripture. When His truth sinks in, the lies quiet down and peace settles in.

My breakthrough came by a river facing the mountains, but yours might come somewhere completely different. Wherever you are, hold on to His truth. That's where you'll find peace.

This past summer I rode through the Rockies again, staring at those peaks that once terrified me. They're still massive, still rugged, still towering above me. But now I see how majestic they are. I'm not small and insignificant anymore. I'm fearfully and wonderfully made, and those mountains remind me how big God is and how deeply He loves me.

I found peace, not in changing the mountains or silencing every voice, but in believing God's truth about who I am. That peace is available to you too.

Freda Neudorf helps women overcome insecurity and create calmer, more organized lives through Time Optimization Coaching. After struggling with her own insecurities, she now coaches others with gentle encouragement. She holds a certificate from The Coach School and lives in Calgary, Alberta with her husband and family. www.abeautifulthing.ca @a_beautiful_thing22

ANCHORED IN PEACE

Tara Norbeck

It was a sweltering August afternoon when I rolled to a stop at a red light. My phone rang. On the other end was my friend and nurse practitioner. Her voice, usually light and cheerful, was low and steady as she spoke the words no one ever wants to hear: *"You have cancer."*

My mind spun. Fear descended like a ton of bricks. Fear of the unknown. Fear of not being able to care for my family. Fear of needing to rely on others. And beneath it all, the deepest fears: fear of pain, and fear of death. Immediately, I felt my life spin out of control. My dad died young of cancer. My mom and her sister battled cancer. *And now me.*

For a long second, time stood still. I gripped the wheel as sweat cooled into a clammy chill. I tried to speak, but my throat closed. The world kept moving, but something inside me had abruptly stopped.

From childhood, I've been a planner, driven by a need to control my life. I love color-coded lists and a well-organized calendar. I often joke that I keep personal planner-makers in business (though honestly, it's probably not a joke). I feel compelled to plan nearly every aspect of my life. A good plan and to-do lists comfort me and ease my anxiety.

Of course, not everything goes according to plan, and my life was no exception. I've experienced many unforeseen detours and had to adapt along the way. But a cancer diagnosis was different. It became immediately apparent that this was not just a bump in the road that I could control.

As both a registered nurse and a mom, I was accustomed to caring for others. A diagnosis of cancer meant the script had flipped. I was suddenly the patient and would have to rely on others for help. That realization shook me, but honestly, what weighed heaviest was my family. They depended on me as the mom who did the grocery shopping, cooked, helped with homework, and ran the carpool. I was the nurse who always played the caregiver role and whom my family looked to for guidance. But I was no longer in control. I was wrestling with casting all my anxiety on him (1 Peter 5:7), only to take it back into my own hands almost immediately after praying.

But unexpectedly, in the middle of my panic, I heard the Lord whisper, *"Trust me."* In that instant, I knew that I had to make a choice—to keep trusting in myself, or to surrender entirely to the Lord by letting go of my plans, my strength, and my control.

Looking back, I know without a doubt that God was with me, even in the moments when I was overwhelmed by fear. Even though He felt far away, He was there the entire time. My diagnosis didn't take Him by surprise. He already knew exactly what I needed, and He had a plan, even as I grasped for control.

The day after that phone call, I was in the surgeon's office. Everything was moving quickly, faster than my mind could keep up. The surgeon was talking, but I didn't hear a word she said. Even so, the bottom line was clear: I would be going in for surgery to remove the mass and lymph nodes in just four days. My head was spinning, yet my heart was strangely beginning to settle. The whisper was becoming louder than the fear and confusion. *"Trust me."*

I wondered aloud if I was experiencing such peace because I was being a Pollyanna, pretending everything was fine. But deep down, I knew this wasn't denial or naive optimism. It was something greater. It was the Lord Himself, comforting me and filling me with the peace of His Holy Spirit.

The more I trusted Him, the louder His voice became. Each time I chose to trust His promises instead of my own fears, His peace settled deeper into my soul. The moment I began to let go of my control and give it back to the One who had held it all along, the Creator of the universe, was the moment peace took root in my heart.

Sweet friend, this is what God does. He knows what you need even before you do, and He waits for you to call on Him. To trust Him. To place your hope in Him so He can flood your heart with His perfect peace, no matter the circumstance. Nothing is too big, or too small, for Him.

God never promised we wouldn't face hardship. Even heartbreak. But He *does* promise His presence, His strength, and His steady hand to hold us. By God's grace, I'm now in remission: a daily reminder that His peace and faithfulness never let go.

"So do not fear, for I am with you; do not be dismayed, for I am your God. I will strengthen you and help you; I will uphold you with my righteous right hand" (Isaiah 41:10).

During this season, my dear friend, Kathy, gave me a bracelet with an anchor charm. I wore it daily—a reminder that God's peace is my anchor. The waves may crash, but His anchor holds. That same anchor can steady you, too. Whatever threatens to pull you under, He invites you to let Him hold you fast in His perfect peace.

If I could leave you with just one thing, it's this: peace doesn't come from wishful thinking that life will get easier, or even from hoping for healing on this side of heaven. True, lasting peace comes only from the Lord, who is faithful in every trial. You can experience this perfect peace, no matter the storms you face, big or small. Turn it over to the One who created you, who loves you more than you can fathom, and allow Him to cover you with His steadfast, perfect peace.

Tara Norbeck, a Texas native, is a wife, mother, and Gigi. She is a registered nurse turned faith-based author and speaker, encouraging others to find hope, healing, and peace through life's challenges. Tara enjoys traveling to places like the beach and Italy, cheering on her favorite sports teams, and spending time with family.

THE OTHER SIDE OF FEAR IS PEACE

Amy Patterson

The breath escapes my lungs and the trembling begins; this is the farthest place from peace. My fear of heights has controlled me for as long as I can remember. I have been trapped in this cage of anxiety for too long. For fifty years I have avoided heights and missed out on opportunities. This visit to Kauai has been tainted with numerous cancelled excursions due to weather. My husband informs me we have only one option remaining to see the Na Pali Coast. With much hesitation I agree to a last minute helicopter tour! Was this a lapse of judgment or a leap of faith?

I climb in, slide the headphones on and muffle the roar of the engine. Sandwiched between the pilot and my husband, I have a front row seat. I am both prayerful and petrified, but there is no turning back now! The pilot's upbeat playlist starts with a nonchalant touch of a button. As I hum along nervously, he interrupts my thoughts: "Everyone ready to go?"

I want to scream "no" but refrain. I know he already senses my fear lingering in these cramped quarters. My heart is racing, palms sweating. The pilot offers a reassuring smile that quickly dissolves into a mischievous grin. He continues, "We are going to have some fun up there!" The propellers roar to life and we lift off. With my eyes safely shut, I feel the ground peel away and as we rise, I feel the helicopter tilt and turn. Much to my surprise, I feel my jaw unclench and my grip on my husband's hand loosen. I let the music and the motion consume me and focus on my breathing.

The pilot nudges me; "Look, over there, a whale!" My eyes fly open. I spot the whale breaching and can't help but giggle at the thought of how large it seemed from earth's perspective and how, from here, it's just a ripple in the water as the whale emerges and dives back in!

Looking up, the vast, vibrant blue sky merges at the horizon with the sparkling sapphire sea. The blues dance together in a spectacular display of color. Up here, the mountains rise out of the earth, every valley and peak is exposed.

Awestruck, I notice the waterfall's grand cascade reaching for miles to the earth's floor. Timed to perfection, the music changes to a familiar movie tune, a living metaphor of the Hollywood scenery God so perfectly created!

The shoreline stretches in a seemingly endless jagged line. Beneath us, large waves ripple like little ribbons to shore. Just above, tiny hikers move cautiously about the cliff's edge. From that same cliff's muddy edge yesterday to this glorious show today, what a gift to see the world from this perspective.

My muscles relax, and a smile grows from my lips. My intense fear has dissolved. I am actually having fun, this is undoubtedly what peace feels like!

We soar through some dark clouds, and rain pelts the windows. As we break free, a spectacular rainbow bursts forth with unimaginably vibrant colors. I feel God's presence, and my heart is full and alive. It is like God has wrapped me in a rainbow of color. My heart is renewed, and my life feels like a fresh canvas awaiting a future masterpiece.

All too quickly, the pilot maneuvers the helicopter to the landing pad, and we gracefully float to the ground. The ride is over but I know my life will never quite be the same.

I want to remember this leap of faith and savor the presence of peace. I am fully aware that trials loom in the future, but now I have experienced the gift of letting go of my fears: God lifting me from my limited perspective. From this day forward I will be flying with God through the storms of life and awaiting the rainbows on the other side. I will not let my fears limit what God is capable of. On the other side of fear is peace. "Here I am." (1 Samuel 3:16)

AMY PATTERSON

"May the God of hope fill you with all joy and peace as you trust in him, so that you may overflow with hope by the power of the Holy Spirit." (Romans 15:13)

Amy Patterson, social worker turned writer, enjoys storytelling and serving as a memoir masterclass story leader. She is on a mission to incorporate mental health awareness in her writing and art. For fun she enjoys photography, travel, kayaking and hiking in Michigan with her husband and dog. author@amypatterson.net

WORSHIP IS THE WAY

Dawn M. Rogers

I sank into my rocking chair as the warmth of the spring sun flooded my patio working its way toward me. Wearily, I stared off in despair. Early mornings are the time of day I intentionally sought God in solitude through prayer, stillness, scripture reading and journaling. Grief crippled me; I couldn't open my Bible or lift my pen. Tears rolled down my cheeks, soaking the lapel of my robe as I thought about the day ahead.

Sobbing, I rocked back and forth. Shards of my shattered heart caused immense pain I had never known. Guttural moans of longing rose from my soul, aching for Olivia, my vibrant, beautiful, 15-year-old daughter who had died by suicide three days earlier.

Sharing Jesus' light, Olivia left a mark everywhere she went. She had a gift with children, earning their trust with ease. As a dancer, she poured her whole heart into every movement. We shared a deep bond and loved doing life together. Her loss reverberated not only through our family, but across the communities she touched: dance, theatre, church, and school.

I grappled with how I could go on without her. In less than two hours my husband and I would walk into Olivia's high school auditorium as 800 students gathered for the morning assembly where the school president would share the devastating news of Olivia's death. I had asked him to share Olivia's favorite verse from Philippians 4:8 "Whatever is true, noble, right, pure, lovely, admirable, excellent or praiseworthy, think of such things" (Philippians 4:8, paraphrased). I knew in my spirit I needed to be there.

My spirit groaned: *Lord, how am I supposed to do this? How can I even stand?*

"I've got you in the palm of my hand, precious. I am with you and will never leave you or forsake you. I am here amid this. I know your heart is shattered. I love you, precious one. I love you," He whispered. I felt His gentle arms help me up.

I shuffled my way back inside to get ready. I brushed my teeth, washed my face, and applied a touch of makeup. In my Spirit, I heard, "I've got you, sweetheart. You're doing it." Out of habit, I opened my phone to a praise and worship station.

Worship through music is my passion. In worship, truth meets me, anchors me and strength begins to rise. I've been a vocalist at my church for decades. My morning routine included listening to worship music, singing along while I got ready for the day. Realizing what I had just done, I muttered, "I'll listen, but I'm not worshipping you."

Then a familiar song filled the room. As the chorus played, each line ministered to my soul, pouring those times of worship back over me like healing balm.

I resisted at first, but soon the lyrics rose from my soul and escaped my lips. Whispering at first, then through weeping, I couldn't help but sing out loud in worship. I closed my eyes and imagined running into Jesus' strong arms to be comforted in His embrace.

I reached out in desperation. At that moment, the Lord met me in an unexpected way. He opened my eyes and gave me a glimpse of Heaven. I saw Jesus carrying Olivia in His arms as a groom carried his bride across the threshold. She sparkled with life and joy. Her face aglow with peace, her brilliant smile and flowing blonde hair shone with a radiance both familiar and heavenly. Her white gown shimmered as she exuded the pure joy of being fully alive in His presence. She wrapped her arms around His neck with one leg lifted high. Her playful delight beamed, reflecting the spirit I had always known on earth. Her smile seemed to say, "Look at me, Mama! Look at me!"—full of life, wonder, and the peace of being safe in His arms.

I broke. "I love you, Olivia!" I sobbed aloud. "I love you so much!"

"I know. I love you, too, mama!" I heard her voice with a vibrancy and assuredness that captivated my entire being.

Then Jesus whispered to me, *She can hear you now, and she believes you! She knows.* I trembled, held in the overwhelming reality of this holy intervention breaking through my despair. The truth of His whisper penetrated my soul.

I had received a precious gift through this divine encounter. I experienced the holy collision of grief and glory in the same breath. Again, words rose like a volcano, burning to be released, yet tangled in my emotions. "I love you, Olivia! I miss you so much!"

Peace flooded my spirit. The Father had lifted me, steadied me, and given me what I needed to face the day. Joy. Strength. Revival.

With a renewed spirit I joined Mark, and an hour later we sat with the students as they heard the tragic news. Following the assembly, I spoke with dozens of inconsolable students. One by one I wiped their tears, looked into their devastated faces, and reminded them of the truth of Jesus' love and sacrifice for eternal life. As a conduit of Jesus' strength and peace, what I had received through worship flowed through me to countless students.

What I experienced that morning in an intimate encounter with God and Olivia gave me a glimpse of eternity and the assurance of her forever in His presence. The first of many assurances, God continues to meet me in my grief with peace that surpasses all understanding.

Even now, years later, when the longing for my precious daughter is too hard to bear, I return to that vision. Jesus' strong arms that welcomed and held Olivia as a bride are tender and comforting, open to me. I accept His warm embrace and rest safely in peace.

Weaving personal stories with biblical truth, Dawn M. Rogers brings energy, light, and transparency to her ministry as a speaker and author. Through her powerful messages, she inspires resilience, hope, and faith, encouraging others to find courage and strength to LIVe—Live In Victory every day. Visit dawnmrogers. com.

BEHIND THE NURSERY DOOR

Neshe Lee Sloan

The water boils over on the stove as I'm trying to keep the toddler out of the dishwasher. My oldest is complaining because his brother wrecked his LEGO creation and I'm babywearing the youngest because he simply wouldn't be put down. I'm unable to process what is happening because there's too much noise and someone is always touching me. I am drowning in diapers, laundry, and emotions to manage (both mine and theirs). How did I ever think I had this motherhood thing figured out?

Having three kids under the age of four left me frenzied. I thrive in organization, order, and predictability, all of which were illusive to me at this stage. Once I figured out the rhythms of parenting one child, I thought I could just replicate it with subsequent children. I thought that by the third time around, I would be sailing through motherhood. But with that sweet third boy came struggles and doubt.

Our house was chaotic and messy, which only added to the shame I felt. The sink was never cleared out and I was forever playing leap frog around cars, trains, and books. We managed to keep the shoes all in one place, which saved my sanity many days. Still, life felt out of my control.

But the chaos on the outside paled in comparison to the chaos within. *Will I ever get it right? Can I ever measure up? Will I ever feel like I'm succeeding as a parent? I can't be the right person for this. Nothing I do is ever good enough.*

During this season, I was solo parenting in the evenings. Three kids and only two hands: the math didn't math. And the baby wasn't falling asleep. I had a routine that worked beautifully with the older two, despite their differing personalities. But when my arsenal of tactics ran out one day, I used what little creativity I had left in my brain for the day to try something different.

I decided to leave the older two to clean their room unattended so that I could nurse the baby before bed. Exhausted and frustrated, I told the boys not to come into the nursery unless someone was bleeding and shut the nursery door. I turned off the light, clicked on the sound machine, and melted into the recliner. At first, I was worried about what the other boys were doing; were they wrestling, fighting, or running around naked? But then I realized it was the first moment of peace in the entire day. I was able to breathe and snuggle my sweet baby for just a few moments in the cool, dark room.

I was overwhelmed by the waves of motherhood, but one drop of peace calmed the storm within and gave me the strength to finish the day well. Peace can be an overarching sensation, permeating our thoughts and feelings. But it can also come in a pocket of time: a simple drop that gets us through and gives us perspective. Those quiet moments in the nursery were the drops of peace that I craved. It became part of our nightly routine.

No matter what was going on outside the door (and sometimes it got very loud), those few minutes gave me the pause I needed. I emerged more patient and less defeated. My shoulders had relaxed, and some of the tabs in my brain closed out, making way for clearer thoughts. I could be the mom that my boys needed because I took that moment to regroup. The truth is that the Lord met me there and showed me that I was not alone. He was holding me just as I was holding our youngest boy. I didn't need to perform or earn anything. I simply needed to be with Him and He would sustain me.

I had been so focused on what I *wasn't* doing well on this motherhood journey that it was refreshing to recognize that the Lord was present and saw me—in the midst of the random paper pile, socks in the corner, and used tissues on my bedside table.

We know that God is always there, as we've been told since we were kids in Sunday school. Yet the world around us can be so loud that we forget to look for Him. Seek out His presence in the midst of your day.

Find moments where you can pause and receive His peace.

Those moments of pause behind the nursery door restored me and reminded me how essential peace is. Sometimes a drop is all that we need.

 Neshe Lee Sloan writes stories of redemption that help women see God at work in their everyday lives. As a writing coach, she guides women in finding their voice and shaping meaningful, inspiring words. She lives in beautiful North Carolina with her husband of 15 years and their three boys.

DISCOVERING PEACE IN SMALL STEPS OF OBEDIENCE

Monica Steely

I wish I could say I didn't know better, that I was too young, too naive. That I was innocent and didn't know the way the enemy worked. That I didn't understand how to avoid temptation. That I didn't realize it was a bottomless pit I was standing at the edge of, and that I fell into it accidentally instead of diving headfirst.

I wish I could say all of that, but I can't. The truth was, I did know better and could have been an oracle for how much better I knew. The enemy operates in ways that are practically transparent, they're so easily seen through. I convinced myself the pit-falling was unforeseen and unexpected, but the only person who believed that lie was me.

The relationship started the way many do: with total flattery. Something like, "Aren't you a sight for sore eyes?" or other ridiculous cliché that inflated my ego just enough to feel special. It started with flattery, then shifted into vulnerability, relating to each other's difficulties and frustrations, finding camaraderie where we lacked it elsewhere.

And then it shifted from friendship to more. It shouldn't have happened; it wasn't God's best for me. I knew this in my bones.

The relationship lasted just long enough for me to feel unrecognizable. I slipped into a season of isolation, hiding from friendships, from church, from community. I believed that if I stepped into the sanctuary of God in any way, He would tattle on me that I was unequally yoked and He didn't approve. So I withdrew from friends, church, and God Himself. I felt too stained to enter His presence in any form, any fashion.

That time was miserable. I wanted to break free and walk away, but I was weak and didn't feel strong enough; the pull to stay was magnetic. There was a hole in my heart only God could fill, but I was blind to it, and this relationship filled the wound. I was finally chosen, highlighted, selected, and seen. I felt like a first-round draft pick, and that feeling will leave you drunk with infatuation when you let it.

I made my world small, and it was tumultuous. That unending, twisting angst settled deep into the pit of my stomach. Panic seized my throat with both hands when I'd see the emails, the text messages, the flashes of the caller ID. Dread gutted me and I was overwhelmed with the weight of oppression.

But even though I knew it wasn't God's best for me, the thought of leaving felt worse. So I lived in the rocky tension of leaving and staying.

The day finally came when my bones were tired from my flesh and spirit fighting. I was lonely and I missed community. Mostly, I missed Jesus and was tired from all of the running, lying, and hiding. I threw on courage like a well-worn sweatshirt, and drove to a weekly prayer group I'd avoided for weeks.

Normally we'd enter in silence, immediately starting individual prayer. I hoped that was still the case again this night. I kept my hat low and slid into the couch, sat still and didn't dare move. Quietly and desperately I held back tears, pulling my hat down further with every failed attempt.

After a time of pretending to pray with my unread Bible in my lap, a note soundlessly slipped onto the page. It was from someone I hadn't seen or talked to in weeks. With shaking hands, I unfolded the note and read,

> *Monica,*
> *Why are you hiding?*
> *God*

We weren't close; she had no way of knowing the turmoil I had been living through. But immediately, with six compassionate words written on leftover office stationery, my carefully constructed façade crumbled. Sobs burst through my chest as Jesus knelt down next to me in the pit. He simply held out His hand and extended grace and peace with determined love in His eyes.

I wanted it with a desperation that ached, but I knew first I had to do the hard work of walking away to grasp it.

The weeks that followed were filled with the tenderest, kindest, gentlest grace ever experienced from God, and it strengthened me to bring the relationship to an end. It wasn't easy; every step forward was met with several back. But God never condemned me; He never shamed or scolded or tattled or punished me. Instead, He walked ahead and illuminated the way. When I got stuck, He paused and looked back, holding out His hand for me to follow. He wooed me forward little by little with unbelievable kindness and generous encouragement.

I've felt God's peace several times before. I've felt it like a river after pouring my heart out in tumultuous storms. I've felt all was well with my soul after wrestling with depression. Each time it was supernatural, beyond all natural human understanding (Philippians 4:7).

But peace showed up differently this time. It was quiet and meek; it came in stages as I walked forward in slow steps of obedience. It wasn't God's peace that strengthened me to walk away; rather the peace unfolded step-by-step as I relied on His strength to do what felt the hardest to do.

I mustered up courage for the difficult conversation, and put an end to the relationship. I stopped responding to texts, emails, and calls. When the enemy whispered that maybe one lunch wouldn't be dangerous, I prayed instead. Slowly, surely, peace took root, and with every obedient step, it grew strong and solid and holy.

In 1 Peter 3:11, Peter writes that we should, "let him turn away from evil and do good; let him seek peace and pursue it" (ESV). I'm still pursuing peace in many areas, but I've learned that when it feels elusive, maybe, just maybe, there's a step of obedience I need to take first in order to find it.

And maybe there's a slow step of obedience you need to take today, too?

Monica Steely writes about discovering Jesus through honest questions and everyday struggles. As co-founder of the Be Still Be Free podcast, she creates space for vulnerable faith conversations. Published in *Today's Christian Woman* and incourage.me, Monica lives in metro Atlanta with her husband, two kids, and ever-present coffee. Visit monicasteely.com to read more.

THE SOUL'S MANNA

Chermaine Stein

eeks dragged by under the constant shadow of dread. An unseen menace stalking her days and cornering her each night. Weary. Sleepless. The inner chorus chanted: *Be brave. Be strong. Study the scripture. You've got this.*

Until one night, lying in bed, it struck: the crushing weight of a thousand-pound fist pressing into her chest, pinning her to the mattress, stealing her breath, silencing her voice. She cut her eyes to the side, toward the faint silhouette of her husband asleep beside her. From somewhere outside herself, she looked on and thought: *This can kill someone.*

The year was 2013, and she was me.

No one knew my secret. I carried it alone.

Logic said, *You know what to do.*

Accusation hissed, *If you acknowledge something is wrong, you give it power.*

Whispers followed, *Leaders don't struggle like this.*

Then came the dart to the soul: *If you had more faith, you could pray this away.*

I was mentoring others while failing myself.

I knew the scripture. I loved the Word. But when I was pummeled by forces that had crept in unnoticed until they revealed themselves in a panic attack, all I "knew" helped me none. I was scrambling for a "word" in the Word and came up empty.

That night was my only panic attack, the culmination of years of distress. And the beginning of the end. Anxiety didn't disappear overnight, it lingered in sleepless nights and the tightness in my throat. But from that night forward, the unraveling had begun.

A short time later, in desperation I asked a minister friend to pray for me. "Lay hands on me and pray."

"Okay," he said. "What for?"

That's when the words rose, shaky but certain. "I'm afraid."

He looked at me gently. "What are you afraid of?"

My answer, the truest confession I could make: "The next thing."

Menace crowded my mind as I awaited that nameless next thing.

Several months later a prophet sat with me at my breaking point. No oil was poured on my head. No earth shook. But what he told me couldn't have changed things more had a tsunami swept through.

"If you understood how much God loves you, you would never be afraid."

Then he had me write out a prayer that I give to you:

Lord, teach me to accept, believe, and practice, in my everyday living, how much you love me with a depth that throws out my fear. Please activate your Word in my life and on my behalf.

Was that prayer a cure-all? No. It was a beginning. Maybe, like me, you too need a rallying point.

The reality? Everyone battles anxiety in one form or another. It never stays in one place. Ignoring it won't weaken it. Silence strengthens it. Anxiety becomes the cruel companion of lonely days.

Worry, wonder, and doubt. The wondering might be the worst. That baseless "what if." Creating "might happens" and then wondering where God is. Wondering why we don't have peace.

Well, God doesn't give peace to figments of imagination. A scenario where He's not in charge isn't found anywhere in scripture. He gives us peace for the day. It's the soul's manna.

Jesus knew what he was doing when He spoke those words in John 14:27: "Peace I leave with you; … do not let your hearts be troubled, and do not be afraid." What Jesus left us was not a parting gift. It is a legacy of His abiding presence.

For a long time, I didn't understand what His peace was supposed to feel like. I kept waiting for some supernatural goose-bumpy *something* to announce its arrival. I already knew what fear felt like. We all do. But I discovered something that shifted the fight. Put me on top.

Fear is cold. A heaviness in the chest, an icy draft that blows in and settles. Sitting on me, hinting with every breath that something bad was coming. Stay alert. Don't relax. No resting.

But peace? Peace, I learned, feels like nothing. Not emptiness, just the absence of fear. A quiet chest. A steady breath. A calm so still it seems unassuming. The miracle is in the silence where cold once lived.

That was the gift Jesus left behind. Not a peace the world shouts about, but His peace. The kind that makes fear lose its grip and steadies your breath when the next thing comes.

Yes, but how?

Pointing out what is wrong does no good if we're not given tools to fight back. Anxiety may be common, but it doesn't have to be permanent. One of my deepest takeaways from that struggle is this: if I have anything to do with it, no one will ever be as old as I was before they break free from the same struggle that gripped me.

Asking for prayer and confessing fear is not "weakness." It is the beginning of a deeper walk with God. I learned to hit back with the Word as my weapon. I applied Romans 12:2 (transformation by mind renewing) with intent, not habit. Taking every thought captive (2 Corinthians 10:5) became a lifeline, anchoring me when fear prowled.

Psalm 18:11 became my touchstone: "He made darkness his covering…" I came to understand that the unknown wasn't something to fear; it is God's garment, a sign He is already on the move. God uses darkness. Darkness never uses God. That truth settled inside of me like the sword it is meant to be. Let it remind you that you are not an unattended ward. You are God's child.

I am not the same woman who lay in that bed in 2013, pinned and breathless. I found the weapon of confession, the power of scripture, and the gift of peace. And so can you.

Jesus left us peace knowing we would need it. Anxiety may shadow some days, but it cannot rule when peace is present. Peace is our legacy. Claim yours.

 Chermaine (Cher) Stein is a content and copy editor, writing coach, and indie publishing consultant. She helps writers clarify their message, strengthen their voice, and share their stories with confidence. Cher is passionate about guiding others toward peace, purpose, and a deeper walk with God.

HOW LETTING GO LED ME HOME

Audrey Tebbe

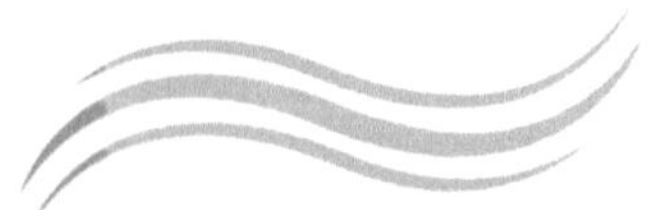

I found myself at a crossroads. The dawn of another Monday morning brought a quiet, heavy dread, like early morning fog blanketing an unfamiliar road. There was no denying that my life needed a different direction.

How did I get here? The career path that had once energized and sustained me now felt confusing and unbearable. How could I have spent so many years achieving, only to wake up feeling empty? The only thing worse than the thought of leaving it all behind was the thought of staying. Something had to change, but walking away felt impossible.

I had poured everything I had into my corporate career. I climbed the ladder, pushed through long hours and weekends, and drove a 132-mile commute each day. Every hour I worked and every mile I drove seemed to measure my worth. Exhaustion and burnout soon became my new companions. My body was waving a white flag I kept ignoring.

Late one evening, after an exhausting week, I fell asleep at the wheel on my way home. I woke up upside down in a ditch, shattered glass around me, my car totaled and my head spinning. As I lay strapped to a stretcher in the emergency room, still shivering from the cold March night, I remember thinking how tired I would be at work the next day. Even with my body in pain, the thought of missing work never crossed my mind.

Moments later, the doctor said that a helicopter was on its way to airlift me to another hospital. My neck was broken in two places. Six ribs were fractured. My lung was punctured, and my liver was bleeding. Surely she wasn't talking about me? I was lucky to be alive.

I spent ten uncomfortable weeks at home in a neck brace, sleeping on a foam wedge and weaning off pain meds. Those long days of stillness should have slowed me down, but they only made me more anxious to get back to feeling like I mattered. When I finally returned to work, I wish I could say everything changed, but I fell back into the same routine, as if nothing had happened. If I wasn't achieving, I wasn't enough.

For five years, I ignored all the quiet nudges, internal conflict, and sense of a deeper call. I kept my distance from God, chasing my own plans. But He never stopped pursuing me. One day, I sensed Him whisper: *You've fallen asleep again, not at the wheel of your car, but at the wheel of your life.* I finally understood: the Lord kept me here for a reason.

It was time to wake up. To change. To truly live with purpose.

The tension between the safety of my old life and the uncertainty of what lay ahead kept growing. One night, in my tiny apartment, tears streaming, I poured my heart out to God. I begged Him to explain why He was asking me to change everything. Without this career to define me, who would I be? In that struggle, I realized I wasn't just terrified of change: I was scared of losing myself, my identity.

That fear seemed more painful than my car accident. I had worked so hard to hold everything together, but I began to realize I wasn't the one holding anything. Surrender wasn't giving up. It was letting go and finally admitting I needed God more than I needed control.

The Lord began to unravel my plans and reveal a new direction. His invitation was to discover peace that had nothing to do with performance, but peace found in His presence. In time, I loosened my grip and even amid the confusion, peace rose quietly within me. Not from knowing the way but trusting the One who guided me. All I needed to do was take one small step after another.

With each step of faith I took, the Lord affirmed my decisions in ways I never could have orchestrated. As I leaned on Him, His plans unfolded: through community, marriage, motherhood, and work rooted in purpose. Slowly, He rebuilt my life from the inside out.

I've come to realize that true peace isn't found in a perfectly planned life. The Lord knows my beginning and my end, and He doesn't waste anything. His plans are far more beautiful than mine ever were. When I let go, I found freedom in His leading.

As I reflect on that season, these words from Jeremiah 6:16 come alive to me, "Stand at the crossroads and look; ask for the ancient paths, ask where the good way is, and walk in it, and you will find rest for your souls."

Christ, the Prince of Peace, dwells within us. As we walk with Him, peace isn't something we have to chase; it's something we carry with us. It isn't fragile like our emotions but steady like the One who holds us. True peace isn't the calm of our circumstances or the pride of our performance. It's the quiet assurance of His presence. When we seek His good way, His peace brings rest to our souls.

Today I live in peace. Not because everything is sure or easy, but because I know the Lord is with me. My worth no longer comes from what I produce but from Whose I am. Peace is His gift, freely given to those who trust Him.

The Monday mornings still come, but they no longer carry a blanket of dread. They arrive with a gentle reminder that the Lord has replaced pressure and performance with purpose. I no longer ask, "What do I want?" but "What do You want, Lord?" and I am at peace knowing that He holds every detail of my life in His hands.

Now, when I stand at new crossroads, I no longer fear the unknown. I know the Lord is with me, lighting the path as He leads me home.

Audrey Tebbe is a wife, mom, entrepreneur, and creator who loves shaping spaces, stories, and experiences that bring people together. She lives with intention, guided by faith and a desire to notice the quiet, beautiful details woven through everyday life.

HOLY HONESTY

Jen VanKommer

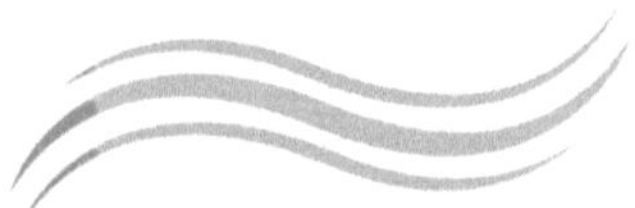

At 19, I am an expert in denial.

Bubbly and positive, I project #blessed with all sincerity. Even I'm convinced that everything's fine.

After all, the evidence is clear: straight-A report card, college leadership roles, raised on church three times a week in a safe, small town. I've known Jesus since the womb.

By every measure, I should be thriving.

Yet here I am, in therapy.

My teenage body has betrayed me: constantly exhausted, always anxious. Although I can't quite pinpoint what's gone wrong, something needs to change.

I'm craving peace.

Still, I start small, offering my therapist surface-level problems with low stakes.

I admit to my constant striving to be "perfect." The latest girl drama in our all-female dorm. An embarrassing interaction with my crush. Typical "good, Christian girl" territory.

Then, as if on cue in a rom-com, comes the therapy cliche: "Tell me about your childhood."

"Are there any wounds there?" my counselor asks. "Trauma?"

I shake my head, "Not really." My parents are still together, moving into their third decade of marriage. No major life upsets or big transitions. Everyone I love is still alive.

But there is that one thing. The painful memory that pops into my head when I least expect it. Taunting me in the middle of a chapel sermon, on a date, just before I fall asleep.

Yes, that memory. The one I need to deliberately shove to the back of my brain where it belongs. *Not today, Satan.*

As a charismatic youth group graduate, I'm convinced the Lord is proud of me for so keenly recognizing this spiritual battle. For taking my thoughts captive and not dwelling on something so negative (2 Corinthians 10:5).

After all, why should I worry? Jesus wins in the end! Surely the most spiritual thing to do would be to let this go.

"There is something," I confess, "but I'm ready to move past that."

My therapist nods knowingly, but gently continues the line of questioning. Delicately, she encourages me to explore this significant memory.

I shift uncomfortably, run my hand across the decorative pillow beside me to buy some time. Finally, when the courage comes, I take a deep breath and start the story.

"I was 9 or 10 years old…"

Suddenly, the resistance hits. I begin to rethink this step of vulnerability.

I don't want to tell this story. It's too painful.

The internal tug of war begins: *Is this really necessary?* versus *Isn't this why I'm here?*

My doubt wins.

I question aloud: "Why can't I just cut off this part of my life? Why even talk about it? It's in the past!"

That's when my counselor tells me something I'll never forget.

"You know that grieving part of you?" she says. "The painful memory you didn't want in your story? It's not going to go away."

I'm stunned. Isn't this Christian counseling? Where's all the talk about victory in Jesus? What about "by his wounds we are healed" (Isaiah 53:5)?

My earliest theology, shaped by itinerant preachers, youth pastors, and my paternal Grandma, hinged on this concept of speaking things "by faith." Never admit to so much as a cold, let alone a serious illness. Smile and "fake it till you make it," even when you want to cry.

As a child, I internalized an unspoken lesson. Living a godly life meant living in denial. Sorrow and lament were not allowed. Grieving was unnecessary.

But on this day, my counselor offers me an image that changes everything.

"By pretending this thing didn't happen," she says, "it's like you're taking a knife and attempting to saw off a part of you. But you can't cut it off. Even if you try, it will always be dragging behind you."

And there it was: the first crack in the "name it and claim it" theology of my youth.

I can't outrun, shove down, or "praise away" my pain. I have never known this until now.

Turns out, grieving was exactly what I needed. It was the antidote to the brokenness I wouldn't even admit I had.

By pretending to be fine, that neglected part of my story would remain limping behind me, a festering wound refusing to heal.

This is the moment I learn to speak honestly about pain. My therapist guides me on this unfamiliar journey of telling the whole truth.

She invites me to name the hurt: "This moment brought me shame." To admit the grief: "I wish this hadn't happened."

Denial, even slyly marketed as "unshakeable faith," wasn't going to heal me. But allowing myself to feel would.

I discovered that God expertly crafted our bodies to feel difficult emotions as a way to release them.

I didn't know that grieving was a path to peace.

At 40, I revisit this revelation. I hear someone describe Jesus as the most emotionally healthy human who has ever lived, and I am captivated anew.

Reading the Gospels with fresh eyes, I witness again and again instances of Jesus expressing real emotions. Our perfect Savior wasn't ashamed to display his disappointment, anger, or sadness. Even Isaiah prophesies that He would be "a man of sorrows and acquainted with grief" (Isaiah 53:3 ESV).

And seeing this truth-telling Jesus, with his raw emotions and zero attempts at pretending, makes the connection between grieving and healing clear.

This radical authenticity makes me fall in love with Him all over again.

The truth is, I am still an expert in denial. "It's all good" is my default.

But now, whenever I lack peace, the distress signal is clear. Anxiety alerts me to deep feelings I'm not expressing. Hard truths I'm avoiding.

Though I've tried dutifully to push them down, I remember it's impossible to cut them off and keep going.

So, I pause and create space. I take the time to name the difficult things and grieve the painful moments. All in the presence of a gentle Savior who understands pain.

Because now I'm convinced: it's holy honesty that ushers in healing and graces us with peace.

Jen VanKommer is a ministry leader and certified spiritual director who creates space for weary hearts to experience God's peace. Though she cherishes memories of serving around the world, her absolute favorite place is snuggled next to her husband, Marcus, and their children. Follow her blog at noticingandnaming. substack.com.

A TRUE HEART REST

Megan Wright

We were in a heated argument. My blood seemed to be pumping through my veins so fast that I could physically feel it moving through my entire body. My heart was racing. I was shaking. I was angry. I was in the midst of speaking angry words while thinking to the Lord, "I can't do this anymore." And it was like the Lord said, "I'm not asking you to. Just trust me and do what I have already taught you." I took a deep breath, shed the tears, wiped them away and dropped to my knees. I put my clenched fists out in front of me, as if I was symbolizing everything I was holding onto. I opened my palms and in that moment I declared surrender of the control of everything and everyone around me that I was holding on so tightly to. It didn't make sense. I didn't have the answers and the other person in that argument with me on the phone was still angry. Nothing was resolved, except the angst in my heart.

Have you ever prayed the prayer "God, would you just please 'fix' them?" I did for years, until the Lord answered with an entirely different response, which had absolutely nothing to do with my question but everything to do with what was really going on in my heart. God nudged me to stop praying for them and start praying for me. I realized in that moment that I had never truly trusted the Lord. I spent much of my life living in cycles of co-dependency, distrust of people, disappointment and exhaustion. Exhaustion from always trying to please others. I longed to be accepted and valued. I wanted people to fill my bucket up because somehow I thought that if people noticed me and affirmed me then I would be satisfied. It was the most damaging lie I've ever believed. And I believed it for so long. The root was insecurity—insecurity with what I looked like, what I was worth, what I could and couldn't do, what I needed help with, what I needed to let go of, what I needed to stop expecting my husband to do that only God could do. That's the void, the emptiness, that I tried to fill most of my life: insecurity. Jesus had to show me that no matter who loved me or who didn't love me here on earth (men, kids, friends, family, co-workers, strangers) I wouldn't feel true, full love until I allowed His ultimate love, His Word, to fill the depths of my heart. I had to discover whose I was and who I was IN HIM. My identity wasn't defined by all the words that I heard from people; it was created and defined by the God of creation. See, the words that stole my peace were the ones that had misplaced value tied to them: value that was superficial and ever-changing, value that was cheap but cost me everything.

So how does this relate to peace? True peace equals rest, and rest equals trust. Rest is surrender. Surrendering our insecurities that fuel our actions is what brings freedom from the need to look for sufficiency in anything and anyone other than Jesus Christ. It's letting go of our expectations for people. It's creating space for the Lord's work to be what we meditate on instead of working to justify our void.

Hebrews 4 actually talks about this. The author references the fourth commandment of keeping the Sabbath day holy. "For anyone who enters God's rest also rests from their works, just as God did from his. Let us, therefore, make every effort to enter that rest" (Hebrews 4:10–11a). He isn't talking about physical rest. Yes, physical rest is important but here he's talking about emotional and spiritual rest that can only come from trusting the one who created it and did it first. God calls us to rest knowing that it's not our works that bring perfection. It's God's work that brought perfection. No matter how much we work, we can't bring the harvest. Only God can. Rest is believing Christ's death was enough. In fact, earlier in Hebrews chapter four, he even says that we should fear not entering the rest of God if we continue to hear the good news of the Gospel and not unite the Gospel with our faith to trust him. True rest is a heart rest. And a heart rest is where you find peace.

I have experienced deep seasons of insecurity, unrest, angst, chaos, anger and pain. But the more I have released others, surrendered others, and let things go, the further away those seasons have become. And now I know that peace can transcend understanding because I'll never understand some people or their actions and words. But I do understand that because I trust in the sufficiency of the Word and how God defines me, I can experience true heart rest knowing that my God has already provided that place of peace for me. And He's already provided it for you as well. He's just calling you to be diligent to enter it.

Megan Wright believes her assignment from God is to equip people to seek Jesus in the messiness of love, with Bible truths, straight talk, and glitter for good measure.